Brand Psychology

Neuro Marketing & Cognitive Psychology, Revolutionising Branding Strategies

Brand Psychology

Neuro Marketing & Cognitive Psychology, Revolutionising Branding Strategies

Sathish Sampath

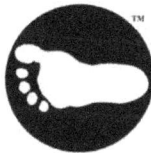

Bigfoot Publications
Because, there's a writer in everyone.

Brand Psychology : Neuro Marketing & Cognitive Psychology, Revolutionising Branding Strategies
Author : Sathish Sampath

First Published by
Bigfoot06 Publications (OPC) Pvt. Ltd.
1st floor, BSR Building near Vishal Mega Mart,
Daultabad Flyover, Laxman Vihar Phase 3,
Gurugram, Haryana (122001)
Website: www.bigfootpublications.in
Email: info@bigfootpublications.in

First Edition : September, 2023
© Sathish Sampath

ISBN Print Book - **978-81-19512-72-0**

Although the author and publisher have made every effort to ensure the accuracy and completeness of information contained in this book, we assume no responsibility for errors, inaccuracies, omissions, or any inconsistencies herein. Any slights on people, places, or organizations are unintentional.

Printed in India

TABLE OF CONTENTS

INTRODUCTION

In the realm of modern business, the synergy between psychology and marketing has paved the way for the dynamic field of Brand Psychology. This chapter serves as a foundational gateway into the intricacies of this discipline, exploring the profound evolution of branding practices and the convergence of psychological insights with marketing strategies. As brands seek to resonate deeply with their target audiences, understanding the evolution of branding and the interplay between psychology and marketing becomes indispensable. This chapter navigates through these critical concepts, setting the stage for a comprehensive exploration of how brands leverage psychological principles to create impactful, resonant connections with consumers.

The Evolution of Branding

"The Evolution of Branding" examines the journey from traditional product-focused marketing to the nuanced landscape of brand-centric strategies. Historically, branding was centered around visual identity, trademarks, and logos. However, as markets grew saturated and consumer preferences evolved, brands shifted their focus to encompass holistic experiences. Techniques such as emotional branding emerged, aiming to forge emotional connections with consumers beyond product attributes. Case in point, Nike's "Just Do It" campaign not only showcased products but also ignited a sense of empowerment and determination. Moreover, experiential branding has gained traction, where brands immerse consumers in memorable interactions. The "Share a Coke" campaign, with personalized bottles featuring individual names, exemplifies experiential branding by creating a personalized experience for consumers.

The Intersection of Psychology and Marketing

"The Intersection of Psychology and Marketing" elucidates how psychology shapes consumer behaviour and decision-making, leading to the synthesis of branding strategies. Psychological theories, such as Maslow's Hierarchy of Needs, have been integrated into marketing models. For instance, Apple's marketing capitalizes on consumers' desire for self-actualization by portraying their products as tools for creativity and self-expression. Additionally, cognitive biases, like the availability heuristic, have spurred innovative marketing techniques. Amazon's "Frequently Bought Together" feature leverages this bias, suggesting complementary products during online shopping. By understanding consumers' cognitive shortcuts, brands effectively influence purchasing decisions.

FOUNDATIONS OF NEURO MARKETING

Understanding Brain Processes in Decision-Making

This chapter lays the cornerstone for a comprehensive understanding of Neuromarketing, a discipline at the crossroads of neuroscience and marketing. We delve into the fundamental principles, methodologies, and applications that underpin this dynamic field. Neuromarketing explores the intricate workings of the human brain, unraveling the subconscious drivers that shape consumer behaviour and decision-making. By fusing advanced technologies with psychological insights, brands can unlock deeper consumer insights and refine their strategies for maximum impact. We will examine the neurological processes behind consumer preferences, emotions, and reactions to stimuli, shedding light on how brands can craft resonant experiences that leave lasting impressions. Throughout this chapter, real-world examples, including the use of functional magnetic resonance imaging (fMRI) to analyse consumer responses, will illuminate the practical applications of Neuromarketing. By delving into the foundational principles of Neuromarketing, readers will gain the tools to navigate the intricate landscape of consumer psychology, equipping them to design strategies that forge profound connections between brands and their audiences.

Neuronal Pathways in Decision-Making: From Stimulus to Response

Neuronal pathways in decision-making elucidate the intricate neural processes that occur from the moment a stimulus is encountered to the subsequent behavioural response. This concept is grounded in the neuroscientific understanding that decision-making involves complex interactions between various brain regions, neurotransmitters, and cognitive processes. When a stimulus is presented, sensory information is transmitted to the brain, triggering neural activation. The thalamus relays this information to relevant brain areas, such as the amygdala for emotional processing and the prefrontal cortex for higher-order cognitive analysis.

Within this framework, various models and theories provide insights into the mechanisms that guide decision-making (detailed explanations and discussions of each theory/model are provided in respective upcoming chapters):

1. **Dual-Process Theory:** This theory proposes two distinct cognitive processes—System 1 (intuitive, automatic) and System 2 (reflective, deliberative)—that collaborate in decision-making. System 1 relies on neuronal shortcuts and heuristics, while System 2 engages analytical and rational thinking. Brands often target System 1 through emotional appeals, tapping into rapid, subconscious responses.

2. **Neuroeconomics:** This interdisciplinary field merges economics and neuroscience to understand decision-making in terms of neural processes. The Prospect

Theory, an influential model in neuroeconomics, suggests that people evaluate potential outcomes based on perceived gains and losses, demonstrating the influence of neural pathways on risk perception.

3. **Neural Reward Pathway:** Decision-making is closely linked to the brain's reward pathway, involving neurotransmitters like dopamine. This pathway is crucial for assessing value and motivating actions. Brands leverage this pathway through incentive-based marketing strategies to trigger positive responses.

4. **Anticipatory Regret Theory:** This theory focuses on the anticipation of regret as a factor influencing decisions. Brain imaging studies have shown that the prefrontal cortex and insula play pivotal roles in processing regret, impacting consumer choices. Brands consider anticipatory regret when designing offers and promotions.

5. **Emotional Influence:** Emotions significantly shape decision-making through the limbic system. Emotional branding techniques, like associating a brand with positive emotions, activate these pathways to enhance brand recall and preference.

Understanding neuronal pathways in decision-making has practical implications for branding strategies. Techniques such as functional magnetic resonance imaging (fMRI) provide insights into real-time neural responses, enabling brands to assess consumer reactions and optimize marketing materials. Furthermore, the application of neuromarketing techniques, such as eye-tracking, can unveil the visual stimuli that influence decision-making.

Neurotransmitters and Their Role in Shaping Preferences

Neurotransmitters and their role in shaping preferences delve into the chemical messengers within the brain that exert a profound influence on consumer decision-making and preferences. These neurotransmitters, such as dopamine, serotonin, and oxytocin, play a critical role in transmitting signals between neurons, modulating emotions, and guiding cognitive processes. The interaction of neurotransmitters with specific brain regions and receptors contributes to the formation of preferences and the evaluation of stimuli.

Several models, theories, and techniques provide insights into the role of neurotransmitters in shaping preferences:

1. **Dopamine and Reward Prediction Error:** Dopamine is central to reward processing and the anticipation of pleasurable outcomes. The Reward Prediction Error theory posits that dopamine neurons fire when an outcome is better than expected, shaping preferences by reinforcing positive experiences. Brands leverage this mechanism by associating their products with rewards to evoke positive associations.

2. **Serotonin and Social Preferences:** Serotonin influences social behaviour and mood regulation. The Social Value Orientation theory suggests that variations in serotonin levels can impact cooperative or competitive behaviour. Brands may consider social factors when designing marketing messages to align with consumers' social preferences.

3. **Oxytocin and Social Bonding:** Oxytocin is linked to social bonding and trust. The Trust Game, used in experimental economics, demonstrates how oxytocin can influence preferences for cooperation or selfishness.

Brands tapping into trust-building strategies can trigger oxytocin release and enhance consumer loyalty.

4. **Neurotransmitter-Targeted Marketing:** Neuromarketing techniques, such as neuroimaging and neurofeedback, enable brands to assess consumers' neurochemical responses to marketing stimuli. By understanding how specific neurotransmitters are triggered by branding cues, brands can tailor messages to elicit desired emotional responses.

5. **Preference Formation:** The mere exposure effect and priming demonstrate how repeated exposure to stimuli can activate neurotransmitter pathways, influencing preference formation. Brands can capitalize on this by consistently presenting their logo or slogan to enhance brand familiarity and preference.

6. **Neurotransmitter-Driven Decision Framing:** Neurotransmitter levels can impact decision framing. Dopamine, for instance, can make consumers more risk-tolerant. Brands can strategically frame their offerings to align with consumers' neurotransmitter profiles, influencing their decision-making.

Understanding the role of neurotransmitters in shaping preferences has strategic implications for brands. By aligning marketing strategies with neurotransmitter-driven responses, brands can create resonant experiences that influence consumer preferences and decision-making. Applying neuroimaging techniques, brands gain insights into consumers' neurochemical reactions, aiding in the design of effective advertising campaigns and product positioning.

In summary, neurotransmitters serve as critical mediators in shaping consumer preferences by influencing emotions, reward processing, and social bonding. Theoretical frameworks like the Reward Prediction Error theory and practical techniques like neurotransmitter-targeted marketing allow brands to tap into these neural pathways, crafting impactful strategies that resonate with consumers and guide their preferences.

Neuroaesthetics: Neural Responses to Visual and Auditory Stimuli

Neuroaesthetics explores the neural responses to visual and auditory stimuli, unraveling how the brain processes and evaluates aesthetic experiences. This concept is grounded in the understanding that aesthetics, encompassing elements like design, colour, and sound, influence consumer perceptions and preferences. By dissecting the neural pathways activated during aesthetic encounters, brands gain insights into designing visually and aurally appealing experiences that resonate with consumers.

Several models, theories, and techniques offer insights into the role of neuroaesthetics (Practical explanation and usage in line with Branding/Neuromarketing is explained in upcoming Chapters):

1. **Aesthetic Appreciation and the Default Mode Network (DMN):** The DMN is a network of brain regions active during introspection and aesthetic appreciation. Activation of the DMN is associated with aesthetic experiences, suggesting its role in processing artistic stimuli. Brands can leverage this by creating visually engaging content that captivates consumers' introspective attention.

2. **Golden Ratio and Visual Harmony:** The Golden Ratio is a mathematical proportion believed to create visual harmony. This principle has been applied across various art forms and design contexts. Brands utilize the Golden

Ratio to achieve balanced and visually pleasing compositions, resonating with consumers' innate aesthetic preferences.

3. **Cross-Modal Correspondence:** This theory suggests that the brain associates sensory experiences across different modalities. For instance, certain shapes may be linked with specific sounds. Brands can capitalize on cross-modal correspondences to align visual and auditory elements, enhancing the overall aesthetic experience.

4. **Neuroimaging Techniques:** Techniques like functional magnetic resonance imaging (fMRI) and electroencephalography (EEG) enable the measurement of neural responses to visual and auditory stimuli. By analysing brain activity, brands gain insights into which elements evoke positive reactions, aiding in strategic design decisions.

5. **Hedonic Value and Aesthetic Pleasure:** The Pleasure-Arousal-Dominance (PAD) model explains emotional responses to stimuli. Brands can enhance consumer experiences by understanding the emotional states elicited by their visuals and sounds, aligning them with desired consumer sentiments.

6. **Brand Consistency and Aesthetics:** Brand consistency in visual and auditory elements fosters familiarity and trust. The Gestalt Principles, such as similarity and continuity, offer insights into how brands can maintain consistent aesthetics across various touchpoints.

Neuroaesthetics holds strategic implications for branding. Brands can leverage neuroaesthetic insights to create compelling visual and auditory content that resonates with consumers' neural responses. By incorporating cross-modal correspondences and applying neuroimaging techniques, brands can align visual and auditory elements, creating holistic and engaging brand experiences. Theoretical frameworks such as cross-modal correspondence and practical techniques like neuroimaging allow brands to design visually and aurally appealing experiences that capture consumer attention and align with their innate aesthetic preferences.

Brain Regions Involved in Brand Perception and Choice

This topic delves into the neurological underpinnings of brand perception and choice, dissecting the specific brain regions that drive these cognitive processes. As brands strive to resonate with consumers on a deeper level, understanding how the brain responds to branding stimuli becomes paramount. By exploring the intricate interplay between neural pathways and branding strategies, this chapter equips marketers with insights into optimizing their approaches for maximum impact. We will navigate through key brain regions associated with brand perception and choice, examining their functions, interactions, and implications for crafting resonant branding experiences.

Associated Brain Regions:

- **Prefrontal Cortex and Brand Evaluation:** The prefrontal cortex, a hub for executive functions and decision-making, critically assesses brand attributes. We will explore how brands capitalize on this region's analytical capabilities to align with consumer preferences and facilitate informed choices. For instance, brands like Apple leverage the prefrontal cortex's rational assessment to emphasize product features and specifications.

- **Amygdala and Emotional Branding:** The amygdala, a key player in emotional processing, shapes brand perception through emotional associations. We will delve into the emotional branding strategies that activate the amygdala, such as Coca-Cola's nostalgic campaigns that evoke emotional connections, fostering brand loyalty by establishing deep emotional ties.

- **Hippocampus and Brand Memories:** The hippocampus, instrumental for memory formation, contributes to brand recognition and recall. We will examine how brands engineer memorable experiences that forge strong associations and trigger the hippocampus for enhanced brand recall. A classic example is McDonald's iconic Golden Arches, etched in the hippocampus through repeated exposure.

- **Insula and Social Perception of Brands:** The insula, implicated in social perception and empathy, shapes the social emotions tied to brands. We will uncover how brands elicit social emotions through compelling narratives, connecting with consumers on a personal level by activating the insula. For instance, Dove's "Real Beauty" campaign resonates by evoking social empathy and inclusivity.

- **Striatum and Reward Processing:** The striatum, central to reward processing, is a driving force behind consumer preferences. We will discuss how brands leverage this region by associating rewards with their offerings, driving consumer choices. Starbucks, for instance, utilizes loyalty programs to trigger the striatum's reward response.

- **Visual Cortex and Brand Visuals:** The visual cortex processes visual stimuli, including brand logos and designs. We will explore how brands strategically optimize visual elements to create distinct brand identities that resonate with consumers. Examples like Nike's iconic Swoosh symbolize the power of visual cues in establishing instant brand recognition.

- **Auditory Cortex and Sonic Branding:** The auditory cortex processes sound, making sonic branding a potent tool. We will delve into how brands harness sonic cues to craft memorable auditory experiences, enhancing brand recognition. Intel's iconic jingle is a prime example of how auditory branding triggers instant brand association.

By dissecting the neurobiology of brand perception and choice, marketers gain the insights necessary to tailor their approaches, aligning with consumers' cognitive responses. The result is a strategic branding framework that captures attention, resonates deeply, and leaves a lasting imprint in the minds of consumers.

Role of Emotions in Consumer Behaviour

This chapter explores the pivotal influence of emotions in shaping consumer behaviour, offering an in-depth exploration of the intricate interplay between emotional responses and purchasing decisions. As brands strive to establish lasting connections with consumers, comprehending how emotions drive behaviours becomes paramount. Within this chapter, we will navigate through the profound impact of emotions on various stages of the consumer journey, from initial awareness to post-purchase satisfaction. By unraveling the cognitive and physiological mechanisms that underlie emotional responses, marketers gain insights into tailoring strategies that resonate deeply and foster brand loyalty.

What we will see in this topic

1. **Emotional Impact on Brand Perception:** We will delve into how emotions colour consumers' perceptions of brands. Emotional branding techniques, such as Coca-Cola's heartwarming holiday campaigns, underscore how tapping into positive emotions enhances brand favourability and association.

2. **Emotion and Decision-Making:** This section uncovers the intricate relationship between emotions and decision-making processes. We will explore how emotions, both positive and negative, influence consumer choices. For instance, the fear of missing out (FOMO) triggers urgency and drives immediate purchasing decisions.

3. **Emotional Triggers in Advertising:** We will delve into the techniques brands employ to evoke specific emotions in their advertising. Examples include Budweiser's emotionally charged Super Bowl ads, which utilize nostalgia and patriotism to create a powerful emotional connection with consumers.

4. **Customer Experience and Emotional Resonance:** This section examines the emotional landscape of customer experience. Brands like Zappos prioritize exceptional customer service to evoke positive emotions, fostering long-term loyalty and advocacy.

5. **Brand Loyalty and Emotional Attachment:** We will explore the emotional attachment consumers develop with brands. Brands that align with consumers' values,

like TOMS' commitment to social responsibility, forge emotional bonds that lead to sustained brand loyalty.

6. **Managing Negative Emotions:** Addressing negative emotions, such as dissatisfaction, is pivotal in maintaining a brand reputation. This section discusses strategies for resolving negative experiences, such as prompt customer support, to mitigate negative sentiments.

7. **Neuroscientific Insights into Emotional Responses:** Incorporating neuroscientific findings, we will unravel the neural pathways that underlie emotional responses. Understanding the brain's reaction to emotional stimuli enables brands to create targeted and impactful emotional experiences.

Emotional Processing and Its Impact on Decision-Making

This section explores the intricate relationship between emotional processing and the choices consumers make, shedding light on how emotional responses shape purchasing decisions and brand preferences.

Emotion and Decision-Making Interaction: Emotional processing is intertwined with decision-making through various cognitive and physiological mechanisms. As consumers encounter products or brands, emotions are evoked in response to cues such as advertising, packaging, or personal experiences. These emotions subsequently influence cognitive evaluations and judgments, thereby directing decision-making.

1. **Positive and Negative Emotions:** Positive emotions, such as happiness or excitement, can trigger an

approach-oriented behaviour, leading consumers to view options favourably and facilitating decisions. For instance, an emotional appeal highlighting the joy derived from using a product can sway consumer preferences. Conversely, negative emotions like fear or anxiety can prompt avoidance-oriented behaviours, driving consumers away from certain options. Fear-based marketing, often employed in health and safety industries, capitalizes on consumers' aversion to negative outcomes to drive choices.

2. **Impact on Risk Perception:** Emotional processing significantly shapes how consumers perceive and evaluate risks associated with decisions. Emotions like fear and uncertainty can heighten the perception of risk, making consumers more cautious and likely to opt for safer alternatives. Brands that address consumers' risk concerns by providing clear information and assurances can effectively mitigate negative emotional influences on decision-making.

3. **Emotional Decision-Making Heuristics:** Emotions also activate cognitive shortcuts, or heuristics, that streamline decision-making. The affect heuristic, for instance, guides decisions based on the emotional valence associated with options. Brands that evoke positive emotions can capitalize on this heuristic, influencing consumers to choose products associated with positive feelings.

4. **Emotion and Brand Loyalty:** Emotional processing fosters the formation of emotional bonds between consumers and brands. Emotional attachment translates to enhanced brand loyalty, as consumers are more likely to choose brands that resonate with their emotional values and experiences. Companies like Apple excel in

fostering this emotional connection, with customers forming strong brand allegiance driven by a sense of identity and community.

5. **The Role of Neuroscientific Insights:** Neuroscientific research reveals the intricate neural pathways that underlie emotional processing and its impact on decision-making. Neuroimaging techniques, such as functional magnetic resonance imaging (fMRI), offer a window into the brain's response to emotional cues, enabling brands to tailor their strategies for maximum emotional resonance.

6. **Practical Implications for Branding:** Understanding the link between emotional processing and decision-making offers profound implications for branding strategies. Brands can leverage emotional appeals in advertising campaigns to trigger specific emotions that align with their products' benefits. For example, luxury brands often evoke emotions of exclusivity and aspiration to influence consumers' decisions.

The Limbic System's Influence on Brand Preferences

The limbic system, a cluster of brain structures, plays a pivotal role in shaping brand preferences through its impact on emotions, memory, and reward processing. Understanding the intricate interplay between the limbic system and consumer choices offers marketers valuable insights into crafting effective branding strategies that resonate with target audiences.

Limbic System's Components and Functions: The limbic system encompasses structures like the amygdala, hippocampus, and nucleus accumbens. The amygdala, responsible for emotional processing, detects salient stimuli and attaches emotional significance to them. The hippocampus encodes and retrieves memories, influencing the context in which brands are encountered. The nucleus accumbens, a core component of the brain's reward circuitry, responds to pleasurable stimuli, such as rewards or positive brand experiences.

Emotion-Driven Preferences: The amygdala's emotional processing shapes brand preferences. Emotionally charged branding campaigns, like Nike's inspirational commercials, activate the amygdala, fostering positive associations with brands. The stronger the emotional connection, the more likely consumers are to develop lasting preferences.

Memory Encoding and Recall: The hippocampus's role in memory encoding and recall influences brand preferences. Brands associated with personal experiences or compelling narratives trigger hippocampal activity, enhancing brand recall. Consider Apple's brand, often linked to innovative design and lifestyle, which forges strong hippocampal connections through consistent messaging.

Reward Processing and Brand Reinforcement: The nucleus accumbens's involvement in reward processing contributes to brand preferences. Brands that deliver enjoyable experiences trigger dopamine release, reinforcing positive associations. Starbucks, for example, creates a pleasurable coffee-drinking ritual that stimulates the nucleus accumbens, fostering brand loyalty.

Neurotransmitter Modulation: Neurotransmitters like dopamine and serotonin, modulated by the limbic system, impact brand preferences. Dopamine, associated with pleasure and reward, amplifies positive brand experiences. Brands leveraging rewards, discounts, or exclusive offers can trigger dopamine release. Serotonin, linked to mood regulation, influences emotional brand connections. Brands fostering a sense of community or social impact, like TOMS, engage the serotonin pathway, nurturing brand loyalty.

Emotion-Driven Decision-Making: Emotions guided by the limbic system influence decision-making. Brands evoking positive emotions align with consumers' goals and desires. By contrast, negative emotions triggered by inadequate customer service can deter preferences. Marriott Hotels' "Golden Rule" initiative resonates with consumers by appealing to empathetic emotions.

Neuromarketing Applications: Understanding the limbic system's influence allows brands to design impactful neuromarketing strategies. Neuroimaging, such as fMRI (extensively discussed in the upcoming chapters), can assess limbic activation in response to branding stimuli. Quantitative data on limbic activity can inform design choices, from packaging to advertising, ensuring emotional resonance.

Formula of Emotional Impact:

Emotional Impact = (Amygdala Activation + Hippocampus Engagement + Nucleus Accumbens Response) × Emotional Valence

---

Example: Consider an advertising campaign by a luxury watch brand that showcases exquisite craftsmanship and timeless elegance. The campaign activates the amygdala due to its emotional appeal, engages the hippocampus by depicting the brand's history, and triggers the nucleus accumbens through the allure of luxury. If the emotional valence is strongly positive, the emotional impact formula yields a high value, indicating a potentially favourable impact on brand preferences.

Emotional Contagion: How Brands Evoke and Transmit Emotions

Emotional Contagion: How Brands Evoke and Transmit Emotions

Emotional contagion, a psychological phenomenon, describes how emotions are transferred from one individual to another. In the realm of branding, this concept explores how brands evoke and transmit emotions to consumers, fostering emotional connections that influence preferences, decisions, and loyalty. Understanding the mechanics of emotional contagion equips marketers with tools to strategically elicit desired emotional responses and create meaningful brand experiences.

- **Emotion Elicitation Strategies:** Brands employ various strategies to evoke emotions. Visual stimuli like colours, imagery, and design elements can trigger emotional responses. Messaging that taps into shared values or personal aspirations resonates emotionally. For instance, a wellness brand promoting holistic health may evoke positive emotions through images of vitality and well-being.

- **The Role of Storytelling:** Storytelling is a potent vehicle for emotional contagion. Narratives that depict relatable challenges and triumphant resolutions evoke empathy and shared emotions. Consider charity campaigns that tell stories of transformation, eliciting emotions of compassion and a desire to contribute.

- **Mirror Neurons and Empathy:** Mirror neurons, neural cells that mimic observed actions and emotions, play a crucial role in emotional contagion. Brands use relatable characters and situations to trigger mirror neuron responses, fostering empathy and emotional alignment with their messaging.

- **Social Proof and Emotional Influence:** Social proof, the tendency to adopt behaviours and emotions observed in others, magnifies emotional contagion. Brands leverage user-generated content showcasing positive experiences to amplify emotional influence. Reviews, testimonials, and social media posts become conduits for emotional transmission.

Formula for Emotional Transmission:

Emotional Transmission = (Elicited Emotion Intensity + Storytelling Impact + Mirror Neuron Activation + Social Proof Influence) × Emotional Resonance

---

Example: Consider a fashion brand's advertising campaign centered on self-expression and confidence. The campaign evokes a strong emotion of empowerment through visuals, employs a relatable narrative of self-discovery, activates mirror neurons by showcasing diverse individuals, and leverages social proof via customer stories. If the emotional resonance is particularly high, the emotional transmission formula yields a significant value, signifying effective emotional contagion.

- **Emotional Brand Alignment:**
o To successfully transmit emotions, brands must align emotional contagion with their core values. Inconsistent emotional messaging can lead to cognitive dissonance, hindering emotional resonance. Brands with a consistent emotional narrative, like Airbnb's emphasis on belonging, establish emotional connections that transcend individual transactions.
- **Cross-Platform Consistency:**
o Consistency across multiple touchpoints amplifies emotional contagion. Brands harmonize emotions

evoked through various channels, ensuring that emotional transmission is seamless.

o Disney's "Happiest Place on Earth" message extends from theme parks to merchandise, nurturing emotional bonds.

- **Measuring Emotional Impact:**
o Assessing emotional impact is crucial. Surveys, sentiment analysis, and focus groups quantify emotional responses. Neuroimaging, like EEG or fMRI, reveals neural reactions to emotional cues, offering quantitative insights into emotional contagion's effectiveness.

- **Neuromarketing Techniques:**
o Neuromarketing leverages insights from emotional contagion to optimize strategies. By tracking consumers' physiological responses to branding stimuli, marketers can fine-tune emotional triggers.

o For example, a travel brand can modify its imagery based on consumers' neural reactions to evoke desired emotions.

Emotional contagion exemplifies the power of emotions in branding. Brands strategically evoke and transmit emotions to create authentic connections with consumers. Employing psychological mechanisms like mirror neurons and social proof, brands craft narratives that resonate, leading to emotional alignment, preference, and enduring loyalty.

Emotion Regulation Strategies for Branding

Emotion regulation, a psychological process, involves managing and modifying emotional experiences. In the realm of branding, understanding and utilizing emotion regulation strategies is instrumental in crafting resonant and impactful brand experiences.

21

This section explores various emotion regulation techniques, theoretical frameworks, practical models, and their implications for branding success.

Cognitive Reappraisal: Cognitive reappraisal involves reframing emotional situations to alter emotional responses. In branding, this technique can be applied by highlighting the positive aspects of a product or service, mitigating negative emotions.

For example, Dove's "Real Beauty" campaign is a prime illustration of the cognitive reappraisal technique in action. The campaign challenges conventional beauty standards by promoting a broader and more inclusive definition of beauty. Dove encourages consumers to reassess their perceptions of beauty and embrace their natural appearances.

Emotion Suppression: Emotion suppression involves inhibiting emotional expressions. In branding, brands may utilize emotion suppression by maintaining a neutral tone to avoid triggering specific emotions. Financial institutions often employ this strategy to convey professionalism and reliability, minimizing emotional fluctuations.

For Example, American Express, a global financial services company, employs emotion suppression as a key element of its branding strategy, particularly in its customer service interactions and communications.

Emotion Selection: Emotion selection entails choosing specific emotions to convey. Brands can select emotions congruent with their messaging.

Examples: A luxury car brand may evoke emotions of exclusivity and sophistication, aligning with its premium image.

Coca-Cola, a global beverage brand, strategically employs emotion selection in its branding to evoke feelings of happiness, joy, and togetherness.

Affect Infusion Model: The Affect Infusion Model suggests that emotions can influence judgments even in situations requiring cognitive processing. In branding, evoking emotions during decision-making enhances brand preference. An emotional advertisement for a travel destination can influence consumers' judgments about the place's desirability

For Example, Nike's "Dream Crazy" campaign effectively employs the Affect Infusion Model by using emotions to influence judgments and attitudes, resulting in a memorable and impactful advertising campaign.

Process Model of Emotion Regulation: This model outlines different stages of emotion regulation: situation selection, modification, attentional deployment, cognitive change, and response modulation. Brands can strategically design experiences across these stages.

Apple's product launches exemplify attentional deployment, with suspenseful presentations creating anticipation.

Emotion Regulation in Customer Service: Emotion regulation is crucial in customer service interactions. Brands can train customer service representatives to use techniques like positive reappraisal to manage customer frustration, ensuring positive experiences and maintaining brand loyalty.

Formula for Emotion Regulation Effectiveness:

Emotion Regulation Effectiveness = (Cognitive Reappraisal + Emotion Suppression + Emotion Selection + Affect Infusion + Process Model Application) × Customer Perception Impact

Example: A fast-food brand aiming to evoke feelings of nostalgia employs emotion selection by associating its menu items with comforting childhood memories. It uses cognitive reappraisal to present its offerings as indulgent treats rather than calorie-heavy meals. If customer perception impact is significant, the emotion regulation effectiveness formula yields a high value, indicating successful emotional engagement.

Neurological Underpinnings: Neuroscientific insights reveal the brain regions involved in emotion regulation. Techniques like cognitive reappraisal activate the prefrontal cortex, implicated in cognitive control. Brands can design messaging that aligns with these neural pathways to facilitate effective emotion regulation.

For Example, Spotify, a leading music streaming service, leverages neurological underpinnings to enhance user engagement through personalized playlists and recommendations.

Individual Differences and Cultural Nuances: Individuals and cultures vary in emotion regulation preferences. Some prefer emotional expression, while others opt for suppression.

Brands operating across cultures must navigate these differences to ensure their strategies resonate universally.

> For Example, McDonald's, a global fast-food chain, demonstrates its understanding of individual differences and cultural nuances by adapting its menu offerings to cater to diverse preferences in different countries, like Veg Aloo Tikki Burger and Veg Maharaja Mac.

Measuring Emotion Regulation Impact: Customer surveys, sentiment analysis, and focus groups gauge the impact of emotion regulation strategies. Metrics like brand preference, purchase intent, and emotional resonance provide quantifiable insights.

Practical Implementation: Brands can implement emotion regulation strategies by aligning emotional cues with their desired brand image. Storytelling, imagery, and language choices should be consistent with the selected emotion. Luxury brands often evoke emotions of aspiration through carefully curated visual and linguistic cues.

Leveraging techniques like cognitive reappraisal and emotion selection, brands can craft experiences that resonate, influence perceptions, and drive consumer preferences. The interplay of psychological theories, practical models, and neurological insights equips marketers to create emotionally engaging brand narratives.

Neuroimaging Techniques for Consumer Insights

Neuroimaging techniques have emerged as valuable tools in the realm of consumer insights, enabling businesses to delve into the subconscious processes underlying consumer behaviour. Leveraging advanced technologies and scientific methodologies, neuroimaging offers a unique window into the human brain, providing unprecedented insights into how consumers perceive, process, and respond to products, brands, and marketing stimuli.

Functional Magnetic Resonance Imaging (fMRI): fMRI is a cornerstone of neuroimaging techniques for consumer insights. This non-invasive method measures changes in blood oxygen levels to map brain activity. By observing brain regions that light up during different stimuli, marketers gain insights into the neural pathways associated with emotions, memory, and decision-making. For instance, fMRI can reveal which brain areas respond when consumers view product packaging, helping brands understand the emotional impact of visual design.

Electroencephalography (EEG): EEG measures electrical activity on the scalp, providing real-time insights into brain dynamics. Its temporal precision allows researchers to examine immediate responses to stimuli. In the context of consumer insights, EEG is used to track brainwave patterns associated with attention, engagement, and emotional arousal. By analysing EEG data, brands can assess the effectiveness of advertisements or user experiences, identifying moments of peak engagement.

Eye-Tracking Combined with Neuroimaging: Integrating eye-tracking technology with neuroimaging enhances consumer insights. Eye-tracking monitors visual attention by recording eye movements, while neuroimaging provides the underlying neural activity. By aligning eye-tracking data with fMRI or EEG, brands gain a comprehensive understanding of not only what consumers look at but also how their brains process those visual cues. This synergy unveils the cognitive and emotional impact of visual stimuli.

Predictive Analytics and Machine Learning: Neuroimaging data can be harnessed for predictive analytics and machine learning models. By training algorithms on neuroimaging responses correlated with consumer preferences, brands can predict how individuals will react to new products or marketing strategies. This predictive power guides decision-making, allowing businesses to tailor their offerings to align with consumer neural responses.

Ethical Considerations and Privacy: As neuroimaging infiltrates consumer insights, ethical considerations become paramount. Safeguarding participants' privacy and ensuring informed consent are crucial. Neuroimaging data is inherently personal and can unveil sensitive information. Brands must adhere to ethical guidelines and communicate transparently with participants about data usage.

Challenges and Future Directions: While neuroimaging techniques offer invaluable insights, challenges persist. Neuroimaging studies require significant resources and expertise, making them relatively inaccessible for smaller businesses. Interpreting complex neuroimaging data demands collaboration between neuroscientists and marketers. Furthermore, the field is dynamic, with evolving methodologies and analyses. As neuroimaging techniques become more accessible and refined, businesses must stay abreast of advancements to harness their full potential.

Functional Magnetic Resonance Imaging (fMRI) in Brand Research :

Functional Magnetic Resonance Imaging (fMRI) has emerged as a potent tool in brand research, allowing businesses to gain profound insights into consumers' neural responses to brands, products, and marketing stimuli. This neuroimaging technique measures changes in blood oxygenation levels in the brain, enabling researchers to map and analyse brain activity with exceptional detail. The integration of fMRI in brand research offers a scientific lens into understanding how brands influence emotions, memory, decision-making, and ultimately, consumer behaviour.

Principles of fMRI: fMRI relies on the principle that neural activity is coupled with local changes in blood flow and oxygenation. The technique detects these changes by exploiting the magnetic properties of oxygenated and deoxygenated blood. When neurons in a specific brain region become active, they require more oxygenated blood, leading to an increased fMRI signal in that region. This signal is then translated into detailed images that showcase neural engagement with various stimuli.

Branding and Brain Activation: fMRI provides insights into the brain regions activated when individuals encounter branding stimuli. For example, when consumers view a brand logo associated with positive emotions, the brain's amygdala (linked to emotional processing) may exhibit increased activity. Similarly, the prefrontal cortex (involved in decision-making) can reveal insights into how branding influences consumers' cognitive evaluation of products or services.

Neural Correlates of Brand Preference: Researchers can use fMRI to investigate the neural correlates of brand preference. By comparing brain activity when participants engage with different brands, researchers can pinpoint the brain regions associated with stronger positive responses. This information guides brands in tailoring their marketing strategies to enhance emotional engagement and preference.

Neural Processing of Brand Elements: fMRI allows researchers to dissect the neural processing of various brand elements. For example, a beverage brand's packaging design might evoke different neural responses based on colour, imagery, and typography. By analysing these responses, brands can refine design choices that resonate most effectively with consumers.

Formula for Emotional Engagement:

Emotional Engagement = (Amygdala Activation + Prefrontal Cortex Engagement) × Emotional Valence

---

Real Example: Starbucks' Brand Experience Study: In a real-world application, Starbucks utilized fMRI to analyse the brain responses of participants engaging with its stores and products. The study revealed that the aroma of freshly brewed coffee triggered heightened activity in brain regions associated with pleasure and positive emotions. Starbucks leveraged this insight to emphasize the olfactory experience in its marketing, enhancing the overall brand perception.

Ethical Considerations: While fMRI offers groundbreaking insights, ethical considerations are paramount. Ensuring participant comfort, informed consent, and data privacy are essential. Participants must be made aware of the potential invasiveness of the procedure and how their data will be utilized.

Challenges and Future Directions: Despite its potential, fMRI is not without challenges. The cost of equipment, expertise required, and data analysis complexity can be barriers. Additionally, fMRI captures neural responses but not the subjective experience, necessitating complementary qualitative research.

Electroencephalography (EEG) and Brainwave Analysis

Electroencephalography (EEG) is a pivotal tool in the realm of neuroscience and consumer insights, enabling researchers to capture and analyse brainwave activity with precision. This non-invasive technique records the electrical activity of the brain through electrodes placed on the scalp. EEG offers a direct window into neural dynamics, shedding light on cognitive processes, emotional responses, and brand-related perceptions.

Brainwave Frequencies and Significance:

EEG captures brainwave activity in different frequency bands, each associated with distinct cognitive states. These frequencies include:

- Delta (0.5-4 Hz): Deep sleep and relaxation
- Theta (4-8 Hz): Creativity, daydreaming, and associative thinking
- Alpha (8-13 Hz): Relaxation, mental clarity, and meditative states
- Beta (13-30 Hz): Active thought, problem-solving, and decision-making
- Gamma (30-100 Hz): Cognitive processing, memory consolidation, and high-level integration

Emotional Engagement and EEG: EEG allows researchers to gauge emotional engagement by analysing brainwave patterns. When participants encounter emotionally resonant stimuli, such as brand logos or advertisements, shifts in EEG frequencies occur. Elevated alpha and theta activity often signal emotional engagement, reflecting attentive and open cognitive states.

Event-Related Potentials (ERPs): ERPs are EEG components linked to specific events, such as stimulus presentation. These responses provide insights into cognitive processes like attention, memory encoding, and emotional processing.

For example, the N170 ERP is associated with facial recognition and can reveal how consumers respond to brand ambassadors or characters in advertisements.

Sensory Processing and Brand Perception: EEG can uncover how consumers process sensory stimuli, informing brand perception. For instance, researchers may analyse the P300 component to explore the brain's response to visual stimuli. If a luxury brand's logo evokes a larger P300 amplitude, it suggests heightened attention and positive associations.

Formula for Emotional Engagement Index:
Emotional Engagement Index* = (Theta + Alpha) / (Beta + Gamma)
*Higher index indicates greater emotional engagement
Example: Pepsi vs. Coca-Cola EEG Study:
A well-known EEG study compared the brain responses of participants to Pepsi and Coca-Cola logos. The study found that the two logos elicited different brainwave patterns, with the Coca-Cola logo triggering more theta and alpha activity, indicative of emotional engagement. This aligned with participants' preference for Coca-Cola in blind taste tests, showcasing the power of EEG in predicting consumer preferences.

Ethical Considerations:

EEG research involves data collection from participants' brains, necessitating stringent ethical considerations. Informed consent, participant comfort, and data privacy are paramount. Ethical guidelines ensure that EEG studies uphold participants' rights and well-being.

Challenges and Future Directions:

EEG studies face challenges in signal noise and anatomical accuracy. Advances in EEG technology and sophisticated signal processing techniques aim to mitigate these challenges. The combination of EEG with other neuroimaging techniques, such as fMRI or eye-tracking, holds promise for more comprehensive insights.

Functional Near-Infrared Spectroscopy (fNIRS) in Consumer Studies

Functional Near-Infrared Spectroscopy (fNIRS) is a cutting-edge neuroimaging technique that holds immense promise in consumer studies. This non-invasive method enables researchers to monitor changes in cerebral blood flow and oxygenation levels in response to various stimuli, shedding light on cognitive processes, emotional engagement, and consumer behaviour. fNIRS has emerged as a valuable tool for brands aiming to decode the neural underpinnings of consumer preferences, decision-making, and brand perception.

Principles of fNIRS: fNIRS operates on the principle that oxygenated and deoxygenated hemoglobin molecules have distinct absorption spectra in the near-infrared range of light. By emitting near-infrared light into the scalp and measuring the reflected light, fNIRS detects changes in blood oxygen levels. This information provides insights into neural activity, as regions of the brain that are more active require increased oxygenated blood supply.

Applications in Consumer Studies: Neural Correlates of Brand Perception: fNIRS can identify brain regions activated when participants view brand logos, advertisements, or product packaging. For example, higher activity in the visual cortex when exposed to a logo suggests strong brand recognition.

- **Emotional Engagement:** fNIRS can track changes in blood oxygenation in regions associated with emotional processing, providing insights into emotional engagement with brand stimuli.

- **Neurological Responses to Pricing and Offers:** Brands can use fNIRS to study participants' neural responses when presented with pricing information or special offers, uncovering how these factors impact consumer decisions.

Example: BMW's Luxury Car Perception Study:

BMW utilized fNIRS to investigate how consumers perceive luxury cars. The study found that participants exhibited higher oxygenated haemoglobin levels in brain areas linked to reward and pleasure when viewing images of BMW's luxury cars compared to non-luxury cars. This insight guided BMW's marketing strategy, emphasizing the emotional appeal of luxury features in their advertisements.

Combining Neuroimaging with Behavioural Data for Deeper Insights

The fusion of neuroimaging techniques, such as functional Magnetic Resonance Imaging (fMRI) or Electroencephalography (EEG), with behavioural data offers a robust framework for delving deeper into the complex interplay between brain processes and consumer behaviour. This interdisciplinary approach allows researchers to bridge the gap between neural responses and real-world actions, providing a comprehensive understanding of how consumers perceive brands, make decisions, and respond to marketing stimuli.

Synergy of Neuroimaging and Behavioural Data:

- **Richer Insights:** Neuroimaging captures neural engagement, while behavioural data records actual responses such as purchase decisions, preference rankings, or engagement levels. Integrating these data sources enriches insights by linking brain activity to observable behaviour.

- **Validating Neural Findings:** Neuroimaging findings are validated by correlating them with behavioural outcomes. For instance, if a specific brain region shows heightened activity during exposure to a brand logo, correlating this activity with positive purchase intent validates the neural response.

Data Integration Process:

- **Experimental Design:** Researchers design experiments that incorporate both neuroimaging tasks (e.g., fMRI scans during brand exposure) and behavioural tasks (e.g., post-exposure surveys or purchasing simulations).

- **Data Collection:** Participants undergo neuroimaging while interacting with brands, advertisements, or product choices. Behavioural data, such as preference rankings or purchase decisions, are also collected.
- **Data Analysis:** Researchers analyse neuroimaging data to identify brain regions associated with specific stimuli. Behavioural data are analysed to discern patterns of consumer behaviour, preferences, or choices.

Advantages of Integration:

- **Neural Basis of Behaviour:** Combining neural and behavioural data uncovers the neurological basis of consumer behaviour. For example, understanding how specific brain regions influence purchase decisions can guide marketing strategies.
- **Personalized Marketing:** Linking neural responses to individual behaviour aids in tailoring marketing campaigns. If a brain response suggests an affinity for certain features, brands can craft personalized messages.

Example: Nike's Ad Campaign Evaluation: Nike combined EEG data and post-exposure surveys to evaluate an advertising campaign. EEG captured participants' neural responses while viewing the ad, revealing heightened theta activity linked to emotional engagement. This neural insight was linked to behavioural data, showing increased positive sentiment and willingness to recommend the brand. Nike leveraged this data to optimize their campaign's emotional appeal.

The convergence of neuroimaging techniques and behavioural data opens an avenue to unravel the intricate relationship between the brain and consumer behaviour. By triangulating neural responses, behavioural actions, and emotional engagement, this approach empowers brands with actionable insights to craft effective marketing strategies, enhance consumer experiences, and ultimately shape the future of consumer research and brand perception.

Implicit and Explicit Memory in Brand Recall

Implicit memory, characterized by subconscious associations and influences, and explicit memory, encompassing conscious recollection, jointly shape consumers' brand perceptions and choices. We explore how these memory systems contribute to brand recognition, preference, and loyalty, and how brands can strategically leverage both implicit and explicit memory processes to create lasting impressions.

Introduction: Implicit and explicit memory mechanisms significantly influence consumer behaviour. Implicit memory operates beneath conscious awareness, impacting preferences without individuals realizing it. Explicit memory, on the other hand, entails deliberate recollection and cognitive effort. Understanding how these memory systems intersect and how they impact brand recall is crucial for crafting effective marketing strategies.

Implicit Memory and Brand Recall: Implicit memory involves associations formed through repeated exposure to stimuli. Brands often capitalize on this by embedding themselves subtly into consumers' minds. For example, the jingle of McDonald's "I'm Lovin' It" triggers implicit memories of the brand, even if consumers aren't consciously thinking about it.

Explicit Memory and Brand Recall: Explicit memory relies on conscious recollection. Consumers actively retrieve information, such as product features, from memory when making purchase decisions. Brands can bolster explicit memory by creating memorable slogans. Think of Nike's "Just Do It" slogan, which consciously connects the brand to a powerful call-to-action.

Neuroscientific Insights: Neuroimaging studies reveal the distinct neural pathways for implicit and explicit memory. Implicit memory tends to activate the basal ganglia, while explicit memory engages the hippocampus. Brands can tap into these neural processes to optimize their advertising strategies. For example, Volkswagen's memorable "Think Small" campaign strategically leveraged explicit memory through its bold and straightforward messaging.

Strategic Implications: Brands can capitalize on both memory systems for effective recall. Implicit memory aids in creating subtle, enduring associations, while explicit memory ensures consumers recall specific attributes. Marketers can craft campaigns that align with both memory types, enhancing brand recognition and loyalty.

Implicit Memory Formation and Brand Association

Implicit memory formation plays a pivotal role in shaping consumers' brand associations, often operating beneath conscious awareness. This subtopic delves into how implicit memory processes contribute to the establishment of brand associations and how marketers can strategically leverage these processes for effective brand recall.

Implicit Memory and Brand Association: Implicit memory involves the unconscious storage of information acquired through repeated exposure. Brands leverage this phenomenon to create subtle, enduring associations in consumers' minds. For example, in the automotive sector, Volvo has built an implicit association with safety by consistently highlighting safety features in its marketing materials.

Theoretical Insights: The mere exposure effect, a psychological phenomenon, highlights how repeated exposure to a stimulus enhances positive feelings and associations. This principle forms the foundation of implicit memory formation. The more consumers encounter a brand, the stronger the implicit associations become. Marketers can capitalize on this effect to reinforce positive brand perceptions.

Explaining Mere Exposure Effect in Detail:

Mere Exposure Effect: Unconscious Favouritism through Familiarity

The mere exposure effect is a psychological phenomenon that highlights how repeated exposure to a stimulus increases an individual's preference and positive feelings toward that stimulus. In other words, the more we are exposed to something, the more we tend to like it, even if we are not consciously aware of the exposure. This effect has significant implications for brand perception, consumer behaviour, and decision-making.

Mechanism and Cognitive Processes: The mere exposure effect operates at a subconscious level, often without individuals being aware of it. When we encounter a stimulus, whether it's an image, a word, or a product, our brain processes it on a basic perceptual level. With each subsequent exposure, our brain's familiarity with the stimulus grows, leading to a sense of comfort and reduced cognitive effort when processing it. This familiarity triggers positive emotions and associations, ultimately leading to a preference for the familiar stimulus.

Application in Branding and Marketing: In the realm of branding, the mere exposure effect plays a crucial role. Brands strive to create memorable and recognizable elements that consumers will encounter repeatedly. This can include brand logos, jingles, catchphrases, and even product packaging. As consumers are exposed to these elements more frequently, they develop a sense of familiarity and comfort, contributing to positive brand associations.

Example: Coca-Cola's Classic Logo: Coca-Cola's classic red and white logo is a prime example of the mere exposure effect in action. Over the years, this logo has been consistently displayed in various contexts, from billboards to TV commercials. As a result of this repeated exposure, consumers develop an innate familiarity with the logo. This familiarity breeds positive emotions and a sense of trust, influencing consumers' preference for Coca-Cola over other beverage options.

Implications for Advertising and Branding: Understanding the mere exposure effect is crucial for advertisers and brand managers. By consistently exposing consumers to brand elements, marketers can create a sense of comfort and positive associations. This is particularly powerful when introducing new products or rebranding, as the more consumers are exposed to the changes, the more likely they are to embrace them.

Limitations and Considerations: While the mere exposure effect is a robust phenomenon, it may not apply to every situation. Overexposure can lead to a point of diminishing returns, where the positive effect plateaus or even reverses. Additionally, the effect is stronger when individuals are not consciously aware of the repeated exposure.

Calculation Technique: Implicit Association Test (IAT) :
The Implicit Association Test measures the strength of implicit associations between concepts. For brand association, the IAT can measure how quickly participants associate a brand with positive or negative attributes. A faster association indicates a stronger implicit connection.

The basic structure of the IAT involves four main categories: two target categories (e.g., "Positive" and "Negative") and two attribute categories (e.g., "Self" and "Other"). Participants are presented with stimuli (words or images) from these categories and are required to rapidly categorize them by pressing specific keys. The test measures the relative ease or difficulty of categorizing stimuli when they are paired in different combinations.

The IAT operates on the assumption that participants will be quicker to respond when stimuli that are more strongly associated in their minds are paired together. This differential response time indicates the strength of the implicit association between the two concepts.

While there isn't a single mathematical formula for the IAT, the data collected from the test can be analysed using statistical techniques to determine the strength of associations and the presence of implicit biases. This often involves calculating response times for different combinations of stimulus pairs and comparing them to infer the strength of associations.

Keep in mind that the IAT is a complex psychological task, and its administration, scoring, and interpretation require careful consideration and expertise in cognitive psychology research methods.

Applying IAT to Brand Association: For instance, an IAT can assess how quickly participants associate a luxury brand like "Louis Vuitton" with "Quality" versus "Affordability."

A quicker association between "Quality" and the brand reflects a strong implicit connection between luxury and quality.

Neuroscientific Perspective: Implicit memory formation involves the basal ganglia, a brain region linked to habit formation and procedural learning. Repeated exposure activates this region, strengthening associations. Brands can tailor their marketing strategies to evoke basal ganglia engagement.

Model: Spreading Activation Theory

According to Spreading Activation Theory, our memory is structured as a network of interconnected nodes, with each node representing a concept or piece of information. When we encounter or think about a particular concept, the activation of that node spreads to other nodes that are closely associated with it. These associations can be based on semantic, conceptual, or experiential connections. The strength of these connections determines how easily information can be retrieved from memory.

Specific mathematical formula, can be understood through the concept of activation strength. Activation strength represents how readily a particular node in the network is activated when a related concept is thought of. Nodes with stronger connections to the activated concept have higher activation strength, making them more likely to be retrieved.

Example: Brand Associations and Spreading Activation Theory

Consider a consumer who thinks about the brand "Apple." In the context of Spreading Activation Theory, this activation leads to the spread of activation to related concepts. For example:

- "iPhone"

- "Innovation"

- "Sleek Design"

- "MacBook"

- "Technology"

Each of these concepts is interconnected with the brand "Apple" in memory, forming a web of associations. The strength of these associations influences how easily the consumer can recall or recognize these concepts when exposed to them. If a marketing campaign emphasizes the concept of "innovation," the activation of this concept can subsequently spread to reinforce the activation of the "Apple" brand in the consumer's mind.

Implications for Branding: Spreading Activation Theory has significant implications for branding strategies. Brands can strategically position themselves to create strong associations with desirable concepts. By carefully selecting and reinforcing the associations they want consumers to make, brands can enhance brand recognition and recall. For instance, a brand that aims to be associated with "environmental sustainability" can strategically create links with concepts like "green," "eco-friendly," and "ethical."

Limitations and Considerations: While Spreading Activation Theory offers insights into memory and association processes, it doesn't provide a full picture of the complexity of cognitive networks. Associations are not always linear, and individual differences can influence the strength of connections. Additionally, real-world brand associations can be influenced by emotional factors, personal experiences, and cultural contexts.

Strategic Implications: Marketers can strategically embed positive associations through repeated exposure and careful brand positioning. Utilizing consistent visual elements, slogans, or music across campaigns reinforces implicit memory formation, enhancing brand recognition and recall.

The Dual-Process Model: Implicit and Explicit Decision-Making

The Dual-Process Model posits that decision-making involves two distinct cognitive processes: implicit and explicit. Implicit processing involves automatic, unconscious, and intuitive responses, while explicit processing involves deliberate, conscious, and analytical thinking. These two processes often work in tandem, shaping consumer decisions in various contexts.

Implicit Decision-Making: Implicit decision-making relies on quick, automatic judgments driven by intuition and emotions. These decisions are influenced by implicit associations, emotional responses, and familiar brand cues. For instance, a consumer choosing a familiar brand of cereal without actively analysing its nutritional content demonstrates implicit decision-making.

Example: Starbucks' Emotional Connection: Starbucks effectively utilizes implicit decision-making by creating a welcoming ambiance and using consistent aroma cues. When a consumer enters a Starbucks store, the aroma triggers positive emotions and familiarity, leading to an implicit decision to purchase, even without conscious deliberation.

Explicit Decision-Making: Explicit decision-making involves conscious analysis, weighing pros and cons, and deliberate evaluations. Consumers engage in explicit decision-making when comparing features, prices, and benefits of different brands or products. For instance, a consumer researching and comparing specifications before purchasing a new smartphone demonstrates explicit decision-making.

Example: Car Purchase Evaluation: When considering a high-involvement purchase like a car, consumers engage in explicit decision-making. They research features, performance metrics, and safety ratings, ultimately making a choice based on rational analysis and comparison.

Interplay and Implications: The Dual-Process Model suggests that both implicit and explicit processes contribute to consumer decisions. Effective branding strategies acknowledge this interplay. Brands can appeal to emotional triggers for implicit responses while providing relevant information for explicit analysis, creating a holistic decision-making experience.

Priming Techniques for Influencing Brand Perception

Priming techniques leverage the influence of prior stimuli on subsequent perceptions and decisions. By exposing individuals to specific cues or information, marketers can "prime" their minds, shaping subsequent attitudes and responses toward brands or products. These techniques tap into cognitive processes to influence consumer perceptions effectively.

Positive Affective Priming: Positive affective priming involves exposing individuals to positive stimuli to evoke positive emotions, subsequently impacting brand perception. For example, a retail brand might use images of smiling faces in advertisements to evoke feelings of happiness, which could lead consumers to associate the brand with positive emotions.

Example: Coca-Cola's Feel-Good Advertisements: Coca-Cola's advertisements often feature scenes of joyful gatherings, celebrations, and friendship. By associating their brand with positive emotions, Coca-Cola primes consumers to perceive their products as enhancers of happy moments.

Semantic Priming: Semantic priming uses words or concepts to activate related associations in consumers' minds. Marketers can strategically use words that are closely associated with desired brand attributes to influence perceptions.

Example: Luxury Car Brand and Elegance: A luxury car brand might employ semantic priming by associating words like "elegance," "refinement," and "prestige" with their brand. By consistently using these terms in their marketing materials, they prime consumers to associate their vehicles with these desirable qualities.

Visual Priming: Visual priming involves presenting images or visual cues that activate specific associations. This technique is particularly effective in conveying brand values and qualities.

Example: Eco-Friendly Brand and Nature Imagery: An eco-friendly brand might use visual priming by incorporating nature imagery, such as lush landscapes or vibrant greenery, in its branding. This primes consumers to associate the brand with environmental consciousness and sustainability.

Priming Effects and Decision Context: Priming effects can extend to various aspects of brand perception, including attitudes, preferences, and even purchasing decisions. Priming techniques can be especially impactful when they align with consumers' needs, desires, and values.

Leveraging Memory Decay and Interference in Brand Communication

Memory decay and interference are cognitive phenomena that impact how memories are retained and retrieved. In brand communication, understanding these concepts can guide strategies to optimize message retention and minimize memory distortion.

Memory Decay: Memory decay refers to the gradual fading of memories over time when they are not actively recalled or reinforced. Brands can strategically use memory decay to reinforce messaging through repeated exposure. Frequent repetition of brand messages can counteract memory decay, helping consumers retain and recall information.

Example: Repetitive Jingles: Brands often use repetitive jingles in commercials to combat memory decay. Catchy jingles, heard repeatedly over time, create a durable memory trace. When consumers hear a jingle on the radio or TV, memory decay is counteracted, keeping the brand and its message fresh in their minds.

Interference: Interference occurs when new information interferes with the retrieval of existing memories. Brands can mitigate interference by ensuring clear and distinct communication, reducing the likelihood of confusion between competing messages.

Example: Clear Brand Positioning: A brand with a clear and distinct value proposition faces less interference. Apple's marketing emphasizes its focus on user-friendly technology. This clarity minimizes interference as consumers can easily retrieve Apple's specific brand attributes without confusion.

Applying Principles: To leverage memory decay, brands should consistently reinforce core messages over time. Frequent exposure helps in retaining key information and brand associations. To manage interference, brands should deliver messages that are distinct and unambiguous, reducing the potential for competing information to distort memory retrieval.

By strategically managing these cognitive processes, brands can reinforce messages, maintain clarity, and ensure that consumers accurately recall and associate desired attributes with their products or services.

Cognitive Biases and Heuristics in Brand Choice

In the realm of consumer decision-making, understanding cognitive biases and heuristics is crucial for marketers. These mental shortcuts and patterns of deviation from rationality significantly impact how individuals perceive and choose brands. Cognitive biases streamline decisions but can also introduce distortions that influence brand perceptions. Heuristics simplify complex problems, aiding rapid judgments. Recognizing these tendencies, brands can strategically tailor messaging, positioning, and product design to align with consumers' cognitive processes. This section explores specific biases and heuristics, including anchoring and adjustment, availability heuristic, confirmation bias, and cognitive reframing strategies. By aligning with consumers' cognitive tendencies, brands can enhance loyalty and guide choices that resonate with inherent biases and heuristics.

Anchoring and Adjustment: The Power of Initial Impressions

Anchoring and adjustment is a cognitive bias where individuals heavily rely on initial information when making decisions, using it as a reference point for subsequent judgments. In brand choice, the initial information consumers receive can significantly influence their perceptions and decisions.

Example: Pricing Strategies and Anchoring: Retailers often use anchoring to their advantage by setting an initial high price for a product before displaying the discounted price. Consumers anchor to the initial high price, perceiving the discounted price as a significant reduction. This technique influences their perception of value and encourages purchases.

Availability Heuristic: Perceived Prevalence Influences Preferences

The availability heuristic is a mental shortcut where individuals judge the likelihood of an event based on how easily they can recall examples. In brand choice, this bias can lead consumers to prefer brands they're more familiar with due to their prominence in memory.

Example: Familiar Brands and Availability Heuristic: Consumers often opt for well-known brands because they are readily available in their memory. Brands that have invested in effective advertising campaigns, appearing frequently on various media, become more accessible in consumers' minds, increasing their likelihood of selection.

Confirmation Bias and Its Impact on Brand Perception

Confirmation bias occurs when individuals seek, interpret, and remember information in a way that confirms their preexisting beliefs or expectations. In brand choice, consumers may selectively attend to information that validates their perceptions, potentially overlooking contradictory evidence.

Example: Product Reviews and Confirmation Bias: Consumers who have a positive preconception of a brand may tend to focus on reviews or information that supports their positive bias while ignoring negative feedback. This confirmation bias can reinforce their existing brand perception.

Overcoming Biases with Cognitive Reframing Strategies

Cognitive reframing involves shifting one's perspective to view situations in a different light, potentially reducing the impact of biases. In brand choice, brands can use cognitive reframing strategies to present information in a way that mitigates biases and influences consumer decisions.

Example: Reframing Product Attributes: If a brand wants to overcome negative biases associated with a particular product attribute, it can strategically emphasize other positive attributes to reframe the consumer's perception. For instance, a brand with a reputation for durability may highlight this strength when introducing a product with a new design.

Anchoring and adjustment, availability heuristic, confirmation bias, and cognitive reframing are essential concepts for brands to understand. By recognizing and leveraging these cognitive tendencies, brands can craft effective strategies that resonate with consumers and guide them toward favourable brand choices.

Multisensory Branding and Crossmodal Perception

Integration of multiple sensory experiences and the understanding of crossmodal perception have emerged as powerful tools for elevating consumer engagement. Leveraging the synergy of various senses allows brands to craft immersive and memorable experiences that resonate deeply with consumers. This section explores how synesthetic marketing, crossmodal correspondences, the impact of soundscapes, haptics, and olfaction, and the art of designing multisensory encounters contribute to the creation of a holistic brand identity. By tapping into the crossmodal nature of human perception, brands can effectively forge emotional connections and establish a unique and compelling presence in the minds of consumers.

Synesthetic Marketing: Merging Senses for Enhanced Branding

Synesthetic marketing involves merging different sensory experiences to create a unified and memorable brand impression. By strategically combining visual, auditory, and tactile elements, brands can evoke stronger emotional responses and create lasting associations.

Example: Starbucks' Sensory Experience: Starbucks provides an exemplar of synesthetic marketing by designing their stores with cozy interiors, soothing colours, and ambient music. This multisensory experience creates an emotional connection that goes beyond the taste of their products.

Crossmodal Correspondences: Symbolism in Sensory Integration

Crossmodal correspondences are innate connections between different sensory modalities, where experiences in one modality trigger perceptions in another. Brands can capitalize on these correspondences to create a cohesive and meaningful brand identity.

Example: Colour and Taste Associations: Crossmodal correspondences are evident in how colour and taste are connected. A brand can leverage this correspondence by using specific colours in packaging that align with the perceived taste of the product, enhancing the overall sensory experience.

The Impact of Soundscapes, Haptics, and Olfaction on Branding

Soundscapes, haptics (touch sensations), and olfaction (smell) play a vital role in shaping brand perceptions. Brands can strategically incorporate these sensory elements to enhance emotional connections and differentiate themselves.

Example: Luxury Hotel Soundscapes: Luxury hotels often use calming soundscapes in their lobbies, enhancing the perception of exclusivity and relaxation. The choice of music and ambient sounds contributes to the desired brand image.

Designing Multisensory Experiences to Enhance Brand Engagement

Creating multisensory experiences involves orchestrating a combination of sensory elements to engage consumers on multiple levels. Brands can use multisensory strategies to create a holistic and immersive brand encounter.

Example: IKEA's In-Store Experience: IKEA effectively designs multisensory experiences within its stores. Shoppers can touch furniture, hear ambient sounds, and even enjoy the scent of freshly baked cinnamon rolls in the cafeteria. This holistic approach fosters a deeper connection to the brand.

Theoretical Insight: Crossmodal Perception and Symbolism

Crossmodal perception theories, such as the "unity assumption," explain how the brain integrates information from different senses to create a coherent experience. Brands can leverage this theory to ensure that sensory elements align harmoniously, reinforcing the intended brand perception.

Model: Spence's Crossmodal Correspondences Model

Professor Charles Spence's research delves into crossmodal correspondences, exploring how senses interact and influence each other. Brands can apply this model to create multisensory marketing campaigns that align with consumers' natural sensory associations. The model suggests that individuals naturally perceive relationships and correlations between sensory stimuli from various senses, even when no direct logical connection exists. These crossmodal correspondences have significant implications for brand perception and marketing strategies. The model posits that certain sensory attributes in one modality can evoke corresponding attributes in another modality. For instance, people tend to associate high-pitched sounds with lighter colours and low-pitched sounds with darker colours. Similarly, individuals may associate certain shapes with specific tastes or textures.

Multisensory branding capitalizes on the interconnected nature of human perception, creating brand experiences that resonate on multiple sensory levels. By employing synesthetic marketing, understanding crossmodal correspondences, harnessing the power of soundscapes, haptics, and olfaction, and designing immersive multisensory encounters, brands can forge deeper emotional connections and establish distinct identities that extend beyond traditional marketing efforts.

Neuromarketing Ethics and Privacy Considerations: Striking the Balance

As the field of neuromarketing continues to advance, it brings forth a series of ethical and privacy concerns that demand careful consideration. Balancing the innovative potential of neuro insights with the responsibility to protect consumer autonomy, well-being, and privacy is essential. This section delves into the ethical dimensions of utilizing neuro data to influence consumer behaviour, the importance of informed consent and participant well-being in neuro studies, and the imperative to safeguard consumer privacy in the realm of neuro marketing research. By addressing these ethical and privacy considerations, brands can ensure that their neuromarketing efforts are conducted with integrity, transparency, and respect for the rights and interests of consumers.

Neuroethics: Balancing Benefits and Potential Harms

Neuromarketing's emergence raises ethical questions regarding its potential impact on consumers' autonomy and well-being. Striking a balance between the benefits of understanding consumer behaviour and the potential risks of manipulation is essential for responsible neuromarketing practices.

Informed Consent and Participant Well-being in Neuro Studies

Respect for participants' autonomy and well-being is paramount in neuromarketing research. Ensuring informed consent, transparency about the research's purpose, risks, and potential benefits, and prioritizing participant safety are crucial ethical considerations.

Ethical Use of Neuro Data for Persuasive Marketing

Ethical concerns arise when leveraging neuro data to influence consumer behaviour. Brands must adhere to ethical standards by responsibly using insights, avoiding manipulation, and ensuring that marketing strategies align with genuine consumer needs and preferences.

Ensuring Consumer Privacy in Neuro Marketing Research

Neuromarketing involves collecting sensitive data about consumers' neurological responses. Ensuring consumer privacy by employing robust data protection measures, obtaining consent for data collection, and providing transparent information about data usage is imperative.

Upholding high ethical standards is not only a legal requirement but also a means to build trust and maintain the integrity of the field. As neuromarketing continues to evolve, it is imperative that ethical considerations remain at the forefront of its practice, ensuring a balanced approach that benefits both brands and consumers alike.

Predictive Modeling and Future Trends in Neuromarketing

Machine Learning and AI in Predicting Consumer Behaviour

Machine learning and artificial intelligence (AI) are revolutionizing neuromarketing by analysing complex data patterns to predict consumer behaviour. These technologies process vast amounts of neuro data to uncover insights that inform targeted marketing strategies.

Example: Netflix's Content Recommendations: Netflix employs machine learning algorithms to predict viewer preferences based on their previous choices. By analysing user behaviour and preferences, the platform recommends content that aligns with individual tastes, increasing user engagement.

Neuromarketing Predictive Models for Campaign Success

Predictive models in neuromarketing use brain data to anticipate campaign success. By correlating neuro responses with consumer preferences, brands can tailor their messaging and strategies to optimize the impact of their campaigns.

Example: Coca-Cola's Super Bowl Ad Campaign: Coca-Cola used neuromarketing predictive models to analyse consumer brain responses to various ad concepts before the Super Bowl. This allowed them to select the concept most likely to resonate with viewers, resulting in a successful and memorable campaign.

Neuroforecasting: Anticipating Market Trends with Brain Data

Neuroforecasting involves using brain data to predict market trends and consumer preferences. By examining neurological responses to stimuli, brands can gain insights into emerging trends and adapt their strategies accordingly.

Example: Tech Gadgets and Neuroforecasting: A technology company might employ neuroforecasting to predict consumer interest in upcoming gadgets. By analysing brain responses to prototypes, the company can gauge excitement levels and anticipate market demand.

The Evolution of Neuromarketing Tools and Techniques

The field of neuromarketing continues to evolve with advancements in tools and techniques. From traditional EEG and fMRI to wearable devices and mobile apps, brands have an array of options to gather neuro data and extract meaningful insights.

Example: Wearable Neuro Devices for Real-Time Insights: Wearable neuro devices allow brands to collect data in real-time as consumers interact with products or experiences. This technology provides immediate insights, enabling brands to fine-tune their strategies on the fly.

Theoretical Insight: Prospect Theory in Predictive Modeling

Prospect theory, a concept from behavioural economics, suggests that individuals value potential gains and losses differently. Brands can incorporate this theory into predictive models to tailor messaging and incentives that align with consumers' risk perceptions and preferences.

Model: Bayesian Belief Networks for Predictive Modeling

Bayesian Belief Networks (BBNs), a powerful probabilistic graphical model, offer a structured approach to understanding and predicting complex relationships between variables. BBNs are particularly valuable in neuromarketing predictive modeling, where various factors influence consumer behaviour and decision-making.

Structure and Function: A BBN consists of nodes representing variables and edges representing probabilistic dependencies between them. Nodes can be observed variables, hidden variables, or outcomes. BBNs capture causal relationships, allowing for the modeling of how changes in one variable affect others.

Application in Neuromarketing: In neuromarketing, BBNs can be used to predict consumer behaviour based on various input variables, such as neuro responses, demographics, and environmental factors. By mapping out the relationships between these factors, brands can anticipate how changes in one aspect might influence consumer decisions.

Example: Beverage Purchase Decision: Consider a BBN used by a beverage company. The nodes could represent variables like consumer age, neuro responses to taste, advertising exposure, and purchase decision. By analysing historical data, the BBN can model how taste perception influences the likelihood of purchase, accounting for the impact of age and exposure to marketing campaigns.

Benefits and Challenges: BBNs offer several benefits, including their ability to handle uncertainty, model complex interactions, and facilitate decision-making under uncertain conditions. However, constructing accurate BBNs requires quality data, domain expertise, and careful consideration of variable dependencies.

Use in Campaign Optimization: Brands can employ BBNs to optimize marketing campaigns. By inputting data about consumer preferences, demographics, and neuro responses, brands can simulate different campaign scenarios to predict which strategies are most likely to yield favourable outcomes.

Advancing Precision in Neuromarketing: As BBNs evolve, they offer a means to enhance the precision of neuromarketing predictions. By incorporating more data sources and refining the relationships between variables, brands can create more accurate predictive models that guide effective decision-making.

By mapping out the complex interplay of variables that influence consumer behaviour, brands can harness BBNs to optimize marketing strategies, enhance campaign effectiveness, and gain deeper insights into the intricate connections between brain responses and consumer choices.

Predictive modeling in neuromarketing, fueled by machine learning, AI, and evolving tools, offers brands the power to anticipate consumer behaviour and market trends. By leveraging brain data, brands can create targeted campaigns, adapt strategies in real time, and stay ahead of emerging trends. As neuromarketing continues to advance, integrating predictive models and future trends can unlock new levels of precision and effectiveness in consumer engagement and brand strategies.

Predictive Modeling and Future Trends in Neuromarketing

The evolution of neuromarketing is driving innovations in predictive modeling, shaping the way brands anticipate consumer behaviour and respond to market dynamics. This section explores key facets of predictive modeling, including the utilization of machine learning and AI to forecast consumer behaviour, the development of neuromarketing predictive models for campaign success, the emergence of neuroforecasting to anticipate market trends through brain data analysis, and the continuous evolution of neuromarketing tools and techniques.

Machine Learning and AI in Predicting Consumer Behaviour : The integration of machine learning and AI technologies into neuromarketing has paved the way for sophisticated predictive modeling. These technologies analyse vast volumes of neuro data to discern patterns and trends, enabling brands to foresee consumer actions and preferences.

Neuromarketing Predictive Models for Campaign Success : Predictive models tailored to neuromarketing offer insights into the potential success of marketing campaigns. By linking neuro responses to consumer preferences, brands can customize strategies that maximize the effectiveness of their campaigns.

Neuroforecasting: Anticipating Market Trends with Brain Data : The concept of neuroforecasting involves extracting insights from brain data to predict market trends. Analysing neurological responses to stimuli enables brands to gain foresight into emerging consumer preferences and market shifts.

The Evolution of Neuromarketing Tools and Techniques : As neuromarketing advances, the tools and techniques available for data collection and analysis continue to evolve. Traditional methods like EEG and fMRI now coexist with wearable devices, mobile apps, and other innovations, offering brands a diverse toolkit to gather neuro data and glean meaningful insights.

Incorporating Theories and Models: The utilization of theories such as prospect theory and models like Bayesian Belief Networks enhances the effectiveness of predictive modeling. Prospect theory from behavioural economics aids in tailoring messaging and incentives to align with consumers' risk perceptions and preferences. Bayesian Belief Networks provide a structured framework for understanding complex relationships between variables in the context of neuromarketing.

Predictive modeling, fueled by machine learning, AI, and cutting-edge tools, represents a pivotal phase in the evolution of neuromarketing. By leveraging brain data to anticipate consumer actions and market trends, brands can fine-tune their strategies and achieve heightened levels of precision in consumer engagement. As neuromarketing continues to progress, the integration of predictive models and future trends empowers brands to navigate the ever-changing landscape of consumer behaviour and market dynamics with greater insight and agility.

COGNITIVE PSYCHOLOGY AND BRAND PERCEPTION

Cognitive psychology serves as a cornerstone in understanding how consumers perceive and engage with brands. This section delves into the intricate cognitive processes that underlie consumer decision-making, exploring topics such as information processing models, attention and perception, encoding and retrieval, and the impact of retrieval cues on brand recall.

Cognitive Processes in Consumer Decision-Making

Cognitive processes lie at the heart of consumer decision-making, orchestrating the journey from exposure to purchase. This section delves into the intricate mechanisms guiding these processes, starting with the information processing models that outline the trajectory of consumer interactions with brands. Attention and perception act as gatekeepers, allowing consumers to filter through the sea of stimuli. Encoding and storage mechanisms shed light on how brands are memorized and recalled, while retrieval cues influence brand recall. As we navigate this exploration, we uncover the cognitive intricacies shaping the choices consumers make and the strategies brands employ to capture their attention and loyalty.

Information Processing Models: From Exposure to Purchase

Information processing models illustrate how consumers move from initial exposure to a brand to making a purchase decision.

AIDA Model: Attention, Interest, Desire, Action

The AIDA model outlines the sequential stages that guide consumer behaviour and decision-making. It stands for Attention, Interest, Desire, and Action. While not a mathematical formula, it provides a structured framework for understanding how consumers move from initial brand exposure to making a purchase decision.

Attention: The first stage involves capturing the consumer's attention. Brands use compelling visuals, striking headlines, or intriguing messages to pique curiosity and create awareness. The goal is to stand out in a cluttered environment and make the consumer notice the brand.

Interest: Once attention is captured, the brand aims to cultivate interest. This stage involves providing more information about the product or service, highlighting its unique features, benefits, and value proposition. Brands often share stories, testimonials, or case studies to engage consumers and keep them interested.

Desire: Building on interest, the brand seeks to create a desire for the product or service. This is where emotional appeal comes into play. Brands showcase how the offering can solve a problem or fulfill a need, evoking a sense of longing or aspiration in the consumer.

Action: The ultimate goal of the AIDA model is to prompt the consumer to take action. This action could be making a purchase, signing up for a newsletter, requesting more information, or any other desired outcome. Brands provide clear calls-to-action (CTAs) and make it easy for consumers to proceed.

Attention and Perception: Filtering Relevant Brand Signals

Consumers are bombarded with stimuli, making attention crucial. Selective attention allows individuals to focus on relevant brand signals while filtering out distractions.

Attention as a Limited Resource: Attention is a finite resource, and consumers allocate it selectively to stimuli that align with their current goals, needs, and interests. Brands compete for this scarce resource, aiming to design messages and visuals that stand out amidst the noise.

Selective Attention and Brand Salience: Selective attention allows consumers to prioritize specific information while ignoring irrelevant details. Brands enhance their salience by using distinct colours, bold visuals, or unique narratives that differentiate them from competitors.

Cognitive Filters and Brand Relevance: Consumers employ cognitive filters to determine the relevance of brand signals. These filters are influenced by factors such as familiarity, personal values, and situational context. Brands that resonate with consumers' existing mental frameworks are more likely to pass through these filters.

Perceptual Vigilance and Inattentional Blindness: Perceptual vigilance involves noticing stimuli that are relevant to one's current needs. On the other hand, inattentional blindness occurs when consumers overlook stimuli that don't align with their current goals, even if they are present in their visual field.

Visual Salience and Brand Design: Visual salience refers to elements that attract immediate attention due to their contrast, size, or placement. Brands strategically utilize visual salience by placing important information where consumers are likely to focus first.

Cross-Modal Attention: Attention is cross-modal, meaning that sensory cues from one modality can capture attention in another. Brands capitalize on this phenomenon by creating multisensory experiences that engage consumers through multiple senses.

Example: Brand Packaging Design

Consider a scenario where a consumer is browsing through a supermarket aisle looking for a healthy snack. In this context:

- **Selective Attention:** The consumer selectively attends to packaging that features keywords like "organic," "low-calorie," and "natural ingredients." These cues align with the consumer's goal of finding a healthy snack.

- **Visual Salience:** Among various packaging designs, a snack package with vibrant colours and a large "100% Natural" label stands out due to its visual salience. The consumer's attention is drawn to this package, influencing their decision.

- **Perceptual Vigilance:** The consumer may overlook packaging designs that don't prominently display health-related cues. Their perceptual vigilance guides them to focus on packages that match their desired attributes.

In this example, attention and perception work together to guide the consumer's choice. The packaging that successfully captures their attention and aligns with their goals has a higher chance of influencing their purchasing decision. Brands strategically design packaging to ensure their signals are not only noticed but also perceived as relevant and valuable by consumers.

Encoding and Storage: How Brands are Memorized and Retrieved

Encoding involves transforming sensory information into memory traces. Storage maintains these traces for future retrieval, impacting brand recall and recognition.

Examples To Understand Better

Encoding Strategies for Brand Recall:

Example: A beverage brand uses a catchy jingle in its commercials, associating the brand name with a memorable tune. This auditory cue enhances encoding as consumers link the brand to the musical element.

Semantic Encoding and Brand Meaning:

Example: A luxury watch brand uses words like "precision," "elegance," and "timeless" in its marketing materials. These semantic cues encode the brand with specific meanings, making it stand out in consumers' minds.

Visual Imagery and Mnemonic Devices:

Example: A fast-food chain's logo incorporates a distinctive shape resembling a smile. This visual imagery creates a mnemonic device, making it easier for consumers to remember the brand by recalling the logo's unique features.

Associative Networks and Brand Links:

Example: A technology brand associates its products with innovation, often depicting futuristic scenes in its advertisements. Over time, consumers create associative networks linking the brand to cutting-edge technology.

Priming and Memory Accessibility:

Example: An electronics brand releases a series of teaser ads before launching a new product. These teasers prime consumers with curiosity and anticipation, increasing the accessibility of the brand's information in their memory.

Chunking and Information Organization:

Example: An e-commerce platform categorizes products into specific sections like "electronics," "fashion," and "home goods." This chunking of information makes it easier for consumers to remember and locate items on the platform.

Levels of Processing and Depth of Encoding:

Example: A car brand's advertisement engages consumers by asking thought-provoking questions about their travel aspirations. This deepens the processing of information, leading to better encoding and retention of the brand message.

Spacing Effect and Distributed Practice:

Example: An online streaming service introduces a new show's episodes over several weeks instead of releasing them all at once. This spacing effect enhances memory retention as viewers anticipate and discuss each episode.

Retrieval Cues and Brand Recall:

Example: A cosmetic brand designs its product packaging with a consistent colour scheme. When consumers encounter the brand's colours in various contexts, these cues trigger recall of the brand's products.

In these examples, encoding and storage mechanisms work harmoniously to create strong brand associations and facilitate effective brand recall. Brands strategically employ various encoding strategies and cues to ensure that their messages are not only memorized but also easily retrieved when consumers engage with products or make purchase decisions.

Retrieval Cues and their Influence on Brand Recall

Retrieval cues trigger memory recall. Brands can strategically embed cues to facilitate consumers' recollection of brand-related information.

Types and Examples of each type of Retrieval Cues

Semantic Priming and Conceptual Associations:

Example: An automobile brand emphasizes the concept of "innovation" in its advertisements. When consumers encounter the term "innovation" in various contexts, it acts as a semantic retrieval cue, prompting them to recall the brand's commitment to advancement.

Context-Dependent Retrieval:

Example: A coffee shop brand creates a cozy and inviting atmosphere in its locations. The environment becomes a contextual retrieval cue that helps customers remember positive experiences they had with the brand.

State-Dependent Retrieval:

Example: A consumer interacts with a brand's website while in a positive emotional state. Later, when they encounter the brand's logo in a different setting, the positive emotional state becomes a retrieval cue, influencing their favourable recall of the brand.

Encoding Specificity and Recall Accuracy:

Example: A fitness brand designs its advertising campaign around the theme of achieving personal goals. When consumers face situations where goal achievement is relevant, the campaign's messages become retrieval cues, triggering associations with the brand.

Cross-Modal Retrieval:

Example: An ice cream brand uses a distinct jingle in its radio advertisements. The jingle becomes a cross-modal retrieval cue that prompts consumers to imagine the taste and texture of the ice cream when they encounter the brand's logo.

Serial Position Effect and Primacy-Recency:

Example: A consumer receives a brochure showcasing various vacation packages. They are more likely to remember the first and last options presented due to the serial position effect. These options serve as retrieval cues for their subsequent decision-making.

Brand Familiarity and Recognition Thresholds:

Example: A cosmetic brand releases a new product line with packaging consistent in colour and design with its existing offerings. The familiarity of the packaging becomes a retrieval cue that helps consumers quickly recognize the new products as part of the brand's portfolio.

Consumer Experience as a Retrieval Cue:

Example: A restaurant brand ensures a consistently exceptional dining experience across its locations. The positive experiences become retrieval cues, encouraging repeat visits as consumers anticipate a similar experience.

Brand Recognition and Recall

Dual Coding Theory and Visual-Verbal Encoding

Dual Coding Theory suggests that combining verbal and visual information enhances memory retention. Brands can utilize this by employing both visual and verbal elements in their communication.

Example: Nike's "Just Do It" Slogan - Nike's iconic slogan "Just Do It" is a prime example of employing the Dual Coding Theory in branding. The slogan combines a concise verbal phrase with a visual logo, creating a dual-encoded representation that resonates with consumers on multiple levels. Nike's use of Dual Coding Theory through the "Just Do It" slogan enhances brand recognition and resonates with consumers across different cognitive pathways. Whether consumers see the Swoosh on products, hear the slogan in advertisements, or encounter it in various media, the combined visual-verbal encoding creates a robust memory representation of the brand's identity and values.

Associative Networks and Semantic Memory Activation

Brands activate associative networks in semantic memory, invoking interconnected concepts and emotions. Well-established brands create robust networks, facilitating recognition.

Example: Coca-Cola's "Share a Coke" Campaign -The "Share a Coke" campaign by Coca-Cola is a vivid illustration of utilizing associative networks and semantic memory activation to foster brand engagement. The "Share a Coke" campaign brilliantly harnessed the power of associative networks and semantic memory activation. By linking the brand to personal names and the act of sharing, Coca-Cola not only evoked positive emotions but also solidified its position as a brand associated with memorable moments and connections.

Brand Familiarity and Recognition Thresholds

Familiarity influences recognition thresholds. Brands with high familiarity are recognized more quickly, showcasing the significance of brand exposure.

Example: McDonald's Golden Arches - When consumers see the Golden Arches logo, their familiarity with the brand activates a range of associations—fast food, affordability, convenience, and the brand's iconic menu items. The high recognition threshold of the Golden Arches logo contributes significantly to McDonald's brand success. It's not just a logo; it's a symbol of comfort food, consistent quality, and a global dining experience.

Enhancing Brand Recall Through Mnemonics and Chunking

Mnemonics and chunking aid recall by organizing information into manageable units. Jingles, slogans, or distinct visuals act as retrieval cues, enhancing brand recall.

Example - FedEx's Hidden Arrow - When individuals recognize the hidden arrow in the FedEx logo, their memory is triggered. This visual element creates a mental connection between the brand and the concept of fast, precise, and streamlined delivery. The hidden arrow in the FedEx logo is a clever mnemonic device that amplifies brand recall. It not only makes the logo visually intriguing but also serves as a constant reminder of FedEx's commitment to timely and efficient service.

The Psychology of Colour and Design in Branding

The role of colour and design in branding extends beyond aesthetics, delving into the realm of psychology and consumer perception. The strategic use of colours, typography, and visual elements holds the power to evoke emotions, establish brand identity, and influence purchase decisions. Understanding the psychological nuances behind colour choices and design elements empowers brands to create visual experiences that resonate with their target audience and communicate their values effectively. In this section, we explore how colour psychology, gestalt principles, typography, and user experience design contribute to shaping brand perception and fostering meaningful connections with consumers.

Colour Psychology: Emotional Associations and Symbolism

Colours evoke emotions and associations. Brands choose colours strategically to communicate specific feelings and brand attributes. When consumers see Starbucks' green logo, their subconscious response is influenced by the colour's emotional connotations. The colour choice reinforces the brand's identity as an ethical and eco-conscious coffee provider.

Gestalt Principles and Visual Perception in Brand Design

Gestalt principles highlight how humans perceive visual elements as unified wholes. Brands apply these principles to create coherent and visually appealing designs.

Example: Amazon's Logo - Amazon's logo capitalizes on Gestalt principles by creating a unified visual that conveys the brand's vast product range and customer-centric approach. The thoughtful application of Gestalt principles in Amazon's logo enhances its recognizability and communicates the brand's commitment to providing a seamless shopping experience from start to finish.

Typography and its Impact on Brand Identity

Typography communicates personality and values. Brands select fonts that align with their identity and evoke the desired emotional response.

Example: Coca-Cola's Script Logo - Coca-Cola's distinctive script logo is a prime example of how typography can be a cornerstone of brand identity. Coca-Cola's script logo serves as a visual representation of the brand's values and emotions. The typography itself conveys the essence of the brand's identity, triggering a sense of familiarity and positive associations.

User Experience (UX) Design and Cognitive Load in Brand Interaction

UX design considers cognitive load, ensuring brand interactions are intuitive and efficient. Brands strive for user-friendly experiences to enhance engagement.

Example: Apple's iOS Interface- Apple's iOS interface prioritizes user experience by designing interactions that require minimal mental effort. The intuitive and consistent design ensures that users can easily navigate and perform tasks without feeling overwhelmed. The user-friendly and efficient UX design of Apple's iOS interface enhances brand interactions. Users associate Apple with ease of use, efficiency, and seamless integration across devices, contributing to a positive brand perception.

Cognitive Biases and Decision Heuristics in Branding

Understanding how individuals make decisions is essential for effective branding. Cognitive biases and decision heuristics are psychological shortcuts that influence our choices, often deviating from rational decision-making. In this section, we delve into how these biases and heuristics shape consumer behaviour and impact brand perception. By recognizing these cognitive tendencies, brands can tailor their strategies to align with consumers' cognitive processes, leading to more informed and effective branding decisions. We explore phenomena like anchoring, confirmation bias, and the paradox of choice, shedding light on their implications for branding strategies.

Cognitive Biases: From Anchoring to Confirmation

Cognitive biases influence decision-making. Anchoring bias occurs when initial information biases subsequent judgments, while confirmation bias leads individuals to seek information that confirms their pre-existing beliefs.

Example: Sale Pricing Strategy - Confirmation bias leads individuals to seek out information that confirms their existing beliefs. Consumers may focus on the positive aspects of a product during a sale while downplaying potential drawbacks. By employing cognitive biases, the sale pricing strategy subtly guides consumers toward perceiving the sale as a significant opportunity. Anchoring and confirmation bias work together to reinforce the idea that the discounted price is a favourable deal.

Prospect Theory and Framing Effects in Brand Preferences

Prospect theory explains how people assess potential gains and losses. Brands frame messages to elicit favourable responses by influencing perceived gains or losses.

Example: Snack Food Packaging - By framing snack packaging in terms of gains and losses, brands influence consumer perceptions and preferences. The framing effect triggers emotional responses that guide decision-making. Snack brands effectively use prospect theory and framing effects to position their products as desirable options. By highlighting potential gains and losses, brands shape consumer preferences and drive purchasing decisions.

The Paradox of Choice: Overwhelm and Decision Avoidance

An abundance of choices can lead to decision fatigue and avoidance. Brands simplify decision-making by offering curated options or recommendations.

Example: Jam Selection Experiment – In a famous jam selection experiment, researchers found that a display with a smaller assortment of jams attracted more attention and sales compared to a larger assortment. When faced with too many options, consumers were less likely to make a purchase due to decision fatigue. Brands that recognize the paradox of choice can tailor their product offerings to prevent overwhelming consumers. By streamlining options and guiding decision-making, brands can enhance the overall shopping experience and boost sales.

Nudging Consumers with Default Options and Decoy Effects

Brands employ defaults and decoy options to guide choices. Defaults leverage the status quo bias, and decoy effects nudge consumers toward a specific choice by introducing less attractive alternatives.

Example: Choice of Meal Portion - By setting default options and introducing decoys, restaurants subtly encourage customers to make specific choices. Consumers often opt for the default or decoyed option without fully evaluating alternatives. Brands strategically employing these nudging techniques can influence consumer decisions in subtle ways. Default options and decoy effects impact choices while maintaining the appearance of variety.

Metacognition and Consumer Self-Perception

Metacognition, the awareness of one's own cognitive processes, plays a pivotal role in consumer decision-making. Understanding how consumers perceive themselves and their thought processes during brand interactions sheds light on their preferences and behaviours. In this section, we delve into the realm of metacognition and its influence on consumer self-perception. By exploring concepts such as metacognitive monitoring, self-concept alignment with brands, and strategies for building self-consistency, brands can gain insights into the dynamic interplay between cognitive awareness and brand choices. This exploration provides valuable insights for crafting branding strategies that resonate with consumers' metacognitive experiences and enhance their brand engagement.

Metacognitive Monitoring and Control in Decision-Making

Metacognition involves monitoring and regulating cognitive processes. Brands can leverage metacognition by guiding consumers' self-awareness during decision-making.

Example: Online Shopping Cart - Metacognitive monitoring prompts consumers to reflect on their intentions, preferences, and perceived value of items in their cart. This reflection informs their final decision to proceed with the purchase or make adjustments. Brands that design user-friendly and transparent shopping experiences that support metacognitive monitoring can enhance consumer confidence in their purchase decisions, ultimately boosting conversions.

Consumer Self-Concept and its Alignment with Brands

Consumers align with brands that reflect their self-concept. Brands create resonance by offering products that harmonize with consumers' identities.

Example - Nike " Just Do it"

Self-Enhancement and Identity Reinforcement through Brands

Brands offer self-enhancement by associating with positive attributes. Consumers seek reinforcement of their identities through brand choices.

Example - Coca Cola "Share a coke" Campaign

Building Self-Consistency and Brand Loyalty

Consumers prefer consistency between self-concept and brand choices. Brands fostering self-consistency enhance loyalty by aligning with consumers' identities.

Example - Starbucks Reward Program

Brand Extension and Transfer of Cognitive Associations

Expanding a brand's presence into new product categories requires careful consideration of how existing cognitive associations and perceptions will transfer to these extensions. This section explores the dynamics of brand extension and the transfer of cognitive associations, delving into concepts such as spreading activation, evaluative conditioning, and the challenges of managing cognitive dissonance during brand stretching. By understanding how cognitive associations are transferred between brands and their extensions, marketers can make informed decisions about brand expansion strategies and navigate the complexities of maintaining brand coherence across diverse product lines.

Spreading Activation and Cognitive Links Between Brands

Spreading activation theory elucidates how activating one concept triggers related associations. Brands leverage this to extend positive associations from one product to another.

Example - Google's Expansion Beyond Search - Google's strong association with internet search and information retrieval naturally extends to products like Gmail and Google Drive. Users perceive these extensions as reliable and efficient due to the positive cognitive links created by Google's search engine.

Evaluative Conditioning: Transferring Affective Responses

Evaluative conditioning transfers emotions from one stimulus to another. Brands evoke positive feelings by pairing their identity with favourable stimuli.

Example - Coca-Cola and Happiness Association - Coca-Cola's branding consistently emphasizes happiness, joy, and sharing moments. By associating positive emotions with its core product, Coca-Cola extends this emotional connection to its various flavors and packaging options.

Cognitive Brand Extensions and Category Fit

Cognitive brand extensions maintain associations by fitting within consumers' mental categories. Brands extend their offerings while ensuring compatibility with existing perceptions.

Example: Apple's Expansion into Wearables - Apple's reputation for sleek design, innovation, and seamless user experiences in the tech world naturally extends to its line of wearables, such as the Apple Watch.

Managing Cognitive Dissonance in Brand Stretching

Brand stretching can trigger cognitive dissonance when the new offering conflicts with existing perceptions. Brands address this by emphasizing related benefits and aligning the new product with the brand's essence.

Example: Porsche's Entry into SUVs - Porsche, known for high-performance sports cars, faced cognitive dissonance when expanding into the SUV market with models like the Porsche Cayenne. Porsche managed cognitive dissonance by ensuring its SUVs maintained the brand's commitment to luxury, performance, and engineering excellence. The company focused on retaining the core Porsche attributes that enthusiasts associate with the brand. By effectively addressing cognitive dissonance, Porsche successfully extended its brand into a new category while preserving its reputation for performance and quality. This strategic alignment minimized the disconnect consumers might feel between Porsche's sports cars and SUVs.

Embodied Cognition and Sensorimotor Influences

Embodied cognition explores the intricate connection between our physical experiences, sensory perceptions, and cognitive processes. This section delves into how consumers' sensory and motor experiences influence their brand perceptions. By understanding how sensory symbolism and physical interactions shape cognitive responses, brands can craft experiences that resonate on a deeper level. Through concepts like embodied simulation and sensory symbolism, this exploration sheds light on how brands can leverage sensorimotor influences to create memorable and engaging interactions that enhance brand engagement and emotional resonance.

Embodied Simulation: Motor Systems and Brand Experience

Embodied cognition links physical sensations with cognitive processes. Brands create immersive experiences by engaging consumers' motor systems.

Example: Tesla's Electric Car Acceleration - Tesla's electric cars offer a unique experience of rapid and smooth acceleration due to their electric powertrains. When drivers experience the immediate and powerful acceleration of a Tesla electric car, their motor systems are engaged. This physical sensation becomes intertwined with the brand's identity, enhancing the perception of cutting-edge technology, performance, and sustainability.

Sensory Symbolism: Linking Physical Sensations to Brands

Brands harness sensory symbolism, associating touch, taste, or scent with abstract attributes. This sensory connection enhances brand perception.

Example: Starbucks and Multi-Sensory Coffee Experience - Starbucks has masterfully linked sensory experiences to its brand. From the rich aroma of freshly brewed coffee to the cozy ambiance of its cafes, Starbucks creates a multi-sensory experience that goes beyond taste alone. When consumers step into a Starbucks, they are enveloped in a sensory symphony of sights, sounds, smells, and tastes. This holistic experience reinforces Starbucks' identity as a premium coffee brand that offers not just a beverage, but an immersive sensory journey.

The Role of Haptic Feedback in Brand Interaction

Haptic feedback engages touch sensations in digital interactions. Brands enhance engagement by incorporating haptic elements into their products and experiences.

Example: Apple's Taptic Engine - Apple's Taptic Engine is a prime example of how haptic feedback enhances brand interaction. The engine provides subtle vibrations and tactile responses to user actions on devices like iPhones and Apple Watches. The Taptic Engine's precision and responsiveness create a unique and consistent tactile experience across Apple's products. This reinforces Apple's brand image of sophistication, innovation, and attention to detail.

Creating Brand Embodiment through Virtual Reality (VR) and Augmented Reality (AR)

VR and AR allow brands to immerse consumers in virtual experiences. Brands facilitate brand embodiment by enabling consumers to interact with brand elements in simulated environments.

Example: IKEA's IKEA Place App - IKEA's IKEA Place app utilizes augmented reality to enable users to visualize how furniture items would look and fit in their own living spaces. Users can place virtual furniture in real-time using their smartphone's camera. The app not only enhances the convenience of furniture shopping but also creates a tangible connection between the user's environment and IKEA's products. This experience deepens brand engagement by allowing users to virtually interact with IKEA items in their own homes.

Neuropsychology of Brand Preference and Loyalty

Understanding the underlying neural processes that drive brand preference and loyalty is a critical aspect of effective marketing strategies. This section explores the neuropsychological foundations of brand attachment, satisfaction, and switching behaviours. From habit formation to reward mechanisms, these topics shed light on the intricate ways in which our brains influence our choices as consumers. By unraveling the neural intricacies of brand relationships, marketers can devise strategies that resonate deeply with consumers' cognitive and emotional responses, ultimately fostering lasting brand loyalty.

Neurological Basis of Habit Formation and Loyalty

Habit formation engages neural circuits. Brands capitalize on these circuits to foster loyal habits through repeated positive interactions.

Example: Starbucks and Habit Formation - Starbucks has cultivated a habit-forming experience by creating a consistent environment, aroma, and personalized beverage offerings. Frequent visits lead to a habitual behaviour pattern that solidifies brand loyalty. By becoming a daily routine for many consumers, Starbucks has built a strong habit-forming brand. The neural basis of habit formation enhances brand loyalty by establishing a neural pathway associated with positive experiences and rewards.

Dopaminergic Reward Systems and Brand Satisfaction

Dopamine drives reward-seeking behaviour. Brands associate positive experiences with their products to trigger dopamine release, fostering brand satisfaction.

Example: Apple's Product Launches - Apple's meticulously designed product launches create anticipation and excitement among its loyal customer base. The unveiling of new products triggers dopamine release, leading to heightened brand satisfaction. Apple's strategic product launches tap into the brain's reward system, eliciting positive emotions that enhance brand satisfaction. This association encourages consumers to associate Apple with pleasure and anticipation.

Neuropsychological Models of Consumer Brand Attachment

Attachment theory explains the emotional bonds between individuals and brands. Brands cultivate attachment through consistent positive experiences and emotional resonance.

Example: Harley-Davidson and Self-Expressive Attachment - Harley-Davidson has built a brand that appeals to consumers seeking self-expression and freedom. The brand becomes a means of expressing individual identity and values. Harley-Davidson's success is rooted in its ability to align with consumers' self-concept. Neuropsychological models help understand how brands like Harley-Davidson forge deep emotional bonds with customers.

Neural Mechanisms of Switching and Churn in Brand Relationships

Neurological mechanisms underlie brand switching and churn. Brands identify and address triggers that lead consumers to switch or disengage.

Example: Spotify's Personalized Playlists - Spotify uses personalized playlists to anticipate users' musical preferences. This proactive approach reduces the likelihood of users switching to other music streaming services. Spotify's data-driven approach minimizes the neural triggers associated with switching by providing a tailored and satisfying music experience, thereby preventing churn.

Ethical Implications of Cognitive Branding Strategies

The integration of cognitive psychology in branding raises pertinent ethical considerations that marketers must navigate. This section delves into the complex landscape where the use of cognitive triggers, behavioural nudges, and psychological insights intersect with ethical boundaries. By exploring the fine line between persuasion and manipulation, transparency in data usage, and safeguarding consumer autonomy, marketers can cultivate strategies that prioritize ethical standards. Balancing the power of cognitive branding with responsible practices ensures that brands engage consumers authentically and respect their decision-making autonomy.

The Ethical Use of Cognitive Triggers in Branding

Brands navigate ethical boundaries when employing cognitive triggers. Responsible use ensures that triggers enhance experiences without manipulating consumer decisions.

Example - Fitbit's Health Tracking - Fitbit encourages users to engage in healthy behaviours by using cognitive triggers like gamification, progress tracking, and social sharing. These elements motivate users to lead healthier lives without coercive tactics. Fitbit's ethical use of cognitive triggers fosters user engagement and loyalty by empowering users to make healthier choices through positive reinforcement and intrinsic motivation.

Nudging for Positive Social Impact: Behavioural Ethics

Behavioural ethics promote nudges that benefit consumers and society. Brands nudge consumers towards healthier choices, contributing to positive societal outcomes.

Example Volkswagen's The Fun Theory Campaign - Volkswagen's campaign encouraged behaviour change by making mundane tasks like using stairs more enjoyable, promoting positive habits. This approach nudges individuals to make better choices without force. Volkswagen's campaign showcases how brands can use nudging techniques to inspire positive change, enhancing the brand's reputation and promoting societal well-being.

Transparency and Consumer Empowerment in Decision-Making

Transparency builds trust by providing clear information. Brands empower consumers by offering transparency about their products and practices.

Example - Patagonia's Transparent Supply Chain - Patagonia openly shares information about its supply chain, manufacturing processes, and environmental impact. This transparency empowers consumers to make informed choices aligned with their values. Patagonia's commitment to transparency builds trust with consumers, strengthening brand loyalty by allowing consumers to align their purchases with their ethical beliefs.

Balancing Persuasion with Consumer Well-being

Brands balance persuasion with consumer well-being. Ethical brands prioritize consumers' best interests by creating value-driven experiences.

Example - Unilever's Dove Real Beauty Campaign - Dove's campaign challenges traditional beauty standards and encourages self-acceptance. The campaign promotes Dove's products while also fostering positive societal change. Dove's approach demonstrates that brands can prioritize consumer well-being while achieving marketing objectives, building long-term positive associations with the brand.

Future Directions in Cognitive Branding Research

The domain of cognitive branding is on a trajectory of ongoing evolution and advancement. This section delves into the potential avenues that research in this field is likely to explore. These include harnessing cutting-edge technologies such as neuropsychological wearables and AI for real-time consumer insights, as well as crafting brands that prioritize cognitive comfort. Embracing these emerging trends will empower marketers to fine-tune strategies that resonate with consumers' changing cognitive dynamics, fostering deeper and more effective brand-consumer connections.

Neuropsychological Wearables and Real-time Consumer Insights

Neuropsychological wearables offer real-time neuro data. Brands gain dynamic insights into consumer responses, enabling agile and data-driven strategies.

Example - Nike's Adapt BB Sneakers - Nike's Adapt BB sneakers use sensors to gather data on wearers' foot pressure and movement. This real-time data informs design improvements, enhancing comfort and performance. Nike's utilization of neuropsychological wearables exemplifies how real-time insights drive innovation, leading to products that align with consumers' cognitive and physical needs.

Cognitive Computing and AI in Customizing Brand Experiences

Cognitive computing and AI personalize brand experiences. Brands utilize algorithms to tailor offerings based on individual preferences and behaviours.

Example - Netflix's Recommendation Algorithm - Netflix uses AI to analyse user viewing habits and preferences, tailoring content recommendations. This personalized approach enhances user satisfaction and engagement. Netflix's AI-driven customization demonstrates how cognitive computing can create personalized experiences, building stronger brand-consumer relationships.

Neuroergonomics: Designing Brands for Cognitive Comfort

Neuroergonomics designs products and experiences for cognitive well-being. Brands prioritize user-friendly designs that minimize cognitive load and enhance engagement.

Example - Herman Miller's Ergonomic Furniture:

Herman Miller designs furniture that optimizes user comfort, posture, and cognitive well-being. Ergonomic chairs, for instance, align with users' physical and cognitive needs. Herman Miller's focus on neuroergonomics emphasizes their commitment to consumers' cognitive comfort, aligning their brand with enhanced well-being.

The Evolution of Cognitive Psychology's Influence on Branding

Cognitive psychology's influence on branding continues to evolve. Brands integrate cognitive insights to create more resonant, engaging, and personalized consumer experiences.

Example - Coca-Cola's Shifting Brand Messaging - Coca-Cola has transitioned its messaging from focusing solely on taste to emphasizing shared experiences and emotions. This evolution taps into the changing cognitive nuances of consumers' perceptions. Coca-Cola's evolution illustrates how brands adjust strategies based on cognitive shifts, enabling them to stay relevant and resonate with consumers over time.

THE POWER OF STORYTELLING

Storytelling is a dynamic and strategic tool that transcends traditional communication approaches. Narratives possess a unique ability to engage, resonate, and influence audiences on a profound level. By weaving captivating tales, brands can create a memorable and emotional connection with consumers, leading to enhanced brand perception, engagement, and loyalty. This section delves into the intricacies of storytelling within the context of branding, exploring how narratives shape consumer behaviour, transmit values, and evoke emotional responses. Through a comprehensive analysis of narrative psychology, emotional engagement, and ethical considerations, this chapter illuminates the transformative impact of storytelling in the modern business landscape.

Narrative Psychology in Brand Communication

Narrative psychology stands at the heart of effective brand communication, shaping how consumers perceive, engage with, and remember brands. Narratives tap into the fundamental human urge for storytelling—a universal means of making sense of the world. In the context of branding, narratives not only convey product attributes but also establish emotional connections and foster brand loyalty. This section delves into the psychological foundations of storytelling, highlighting its role in transmitting culture and values. Additionally, it explores narratives as cognitive tools that assist consumers in comprehending and relating to brands on a deeper level. Moreover, the power of archetypal narratives in branding is examined, illustrating how these fundamental story patterns evoke primal emotions and resonate across diverse audiences. By comprehending the intricate interplay between narrative psychology and brand communication, businesses can craft compelling stories that resonate with consumers and leave lasting impressions.

Psychological Foundations of Storytelling: The Narrative Urge: The narrative urge is an innate human inclination to construct and engage with stories as a means of understanding and communicating experiences. This fundamental cognitive tendency underpins the effectiveness of storytelling in brand communication. Brands that harness the narrative urge tap into a deep well of psychological resonance, as individuals naturally gravitate toward stories that mirror their own lives, aspirations, and emotions. This phenomenon is rooted in the brain's inclination to process information in narrative form, making stories easier to comprehend, remember, and connect with on an emotional level. From ancient myths to modern advertising campaigns, narratives have consistently demonstrated the ability to evoke empathy, shape beliefs, and influence behaviours. By understanding the narrative urge, marketers can strategically craft brand stories that align with human cognitive tendencies, fostering a more profound and lasting connection between consumers and their brands of choice.

Example: Coca-Cola's "Share a Coke" campaign uses personalized labels to encourage consumers to share their stories and experiences with the brand, enhancing brand engagement.

The Role of Stories in Transmitting Culture and Values: Stories play a pivotal role in the transmission of culture and values across generations. Through narratives, societies share their beliefs, norms, and traditions, weaving them into the fabric of collective identity. Brands that recognize this power can leverage storytelling to align themselves with the cultural aspirations of their target audiences. Stories become vessels that carry cultural symbols, enabling brands to establish a sense of belonging and resonance with consumers who identify with the shared values presented in these narratives. By weaving cultural elements into brand stories, marketers can tap into deep-seated emotions and tap into the cultural narratives that resonate with their audience. This synchronization fosters a sense of authenticity and relevance, allowing brands to transcend commercial boundaries and become part of the cultural tapestry that shapes consumers' lives.

Example: Nike's "Just Do It" campaign reflects the brand's cultural values of determination, empowerment, and achievement, resonating with consumers globally.

Stories as Cognitive Tools for Making Sense of Brands: Human minds are wired to process and make sense of information through stories. Narratives provide a structured framework that helps individuals organize and understand complex concepts, including brands. Brands that harness the power of storytelling can create cohesive narratives that guide consumers in comprehending their values, offerings, and unique selling propositions. By presenting brand information in the form of a story, marketers tap into cognitive processes that facilitate better retention and comprehension. These narratives not only make brands more memorable but also establish an emotional connection, allowing consumers to relate on a personal level. Just as characters in a story evolve, brands can use narratives to showcase growth, transformation, and adaptation, thus aligning with the consumer's journey. Through storytelling, brands become more relatable, humanizing themselves and creating cognitive bridges that enable consumers to process and internalize brand messages with greater clarity and resonance.

Example: Apple's origin story, depicting Steve Jobs' journey from a garage startup to a tech giant, assists consumers in understanding the brand's innovation and ethos.

The Power of Archetypal Narratives in Branding: Archetypal narratives are deeply ingrained in human culture and psychology, often resonating with universal themes and emotions. Brands that align with archetypal narratives tap into a collective understanding and evoke powerful emotional responses. By embodying archetypal characters, situations, or journeys in their storytelling, brands establish connections that transcend individual preferences and resonate with a broader audience. For instance, the "Hero's Journey" archetype, popularized by Joseph Campbell, involves a protagonist facing challenges, undergoing transformation, and emerging triumphant. Brands like Nike effectively employ this archetype by positioning their products as tools to help individuals overcome obstacles and achieve personal victories. By aligning with archetypal narratives, brands tap into primal emotions and subconscious associations, creating a sense of familiarity and resonance that drives consumer loyalty and engagement. This approach allows brands to become a part of consumers' personal narratives, resulting in lasting and meaningful connections that extend beyond transactional relationships.

Example: Harley-Davidson leverages the "Rebel" archetype to evoke a sense of freedom and nonconformity, resonating with its motorcycle enthusiasts.

Creating Emotional Connections Through Stories

Emotions are a powerful driver of human behaviour, and storytelling has the ability to evoke profound emotional responses. In the realm of branding, stories play a pivotal role in forging emotional connections between consumers and brands. Through carefully crafted narratives, brands can engage with consumers on an emotional level, fostering empathy, relatability, and a sense of shared experience. This section explores how emotional engagement, facilitated by the neurochemistry of storytelling, creates resonant brand narratives that leave a lasting impact on consumers.

Emotional Engagement and the Neurochemistry of Storytelling: The process of storytelling is not merely about conveying information; it also has a profound impact on our brain chemistry and emotional responses. When we engage with a compelling story, our brains release a cascade of neurotransmitters and hormones that contribute to emotional arousal and connection. This emotional engagement is rooted in the neurochemical interplay of oxytocin, dopamine, and cortisol, which collectively shape our emotional experiences during storytelling. Brands that master the art of crafting emotionally resonant narratives can tap into this neurochemical dance, creating narratives that trigger feelings of empathy, joy, or even suspense, thereby establishing a strong emotional bond between consumers and their products or services.

Example: Google's "Dear Sophie" ad evokes emotions by showcasing a father documenting his daughter's life using Google products, fostering a deep emotional connection.

Mirror Neurons and Empathy: Connecting with Brand Narratives: Mirror neurons, a class of brain cells that fire both when an individual performs an action and when they observe another person performing the same action, play a crucial role in fostering empathy and emotional connection. When it comes to brand narratives, mirror neurons enable consumers to vicariously experience the emotions and experiences depicted in the stories. By activating the same neural pathways responsible for personal experiences, mirror neurons allow individuals to relate to the characters and situations within the narrative. Brands that leverage mirror neuron activation can effectively evoke empathy, resonating with consumers on a deep emotional level. This connection not only enhances brand likability but also promotes a sense of shared understanding and alignment with the brand's values, ultimately contributing to stronger brand-consumer relationships.

Example: Airbnb's "We Accept" campaign narrates real stories of inclusivity, utilizing mirror neurons to create empathy and understanding.

Emotional Arcs and Catharsis in Brand Storytelling:
Emotional arcs in brand storytelling are structured trajectories of emotions that guide consumers through a sequence of feelings, ultimately leading to catharsis—a sense of emotional release and resolution. Brands strategically utilize emotional arcs to create a captivating and impactful narrative experience. Just as in traditional storytelling, emotional arcs in brand narratives often follow a pattern of tension, climax, and resolution. This progression triggers emotional engagement, keeping the audience invested in the story's outcome. Catharsis, the pinnacle of emotional arcs, offers consumers a sense of emotional relief and insight, which can deepen their connection to the brand. This technique is particularly effective when it resonates with consumers' personal experiences and aspirations. By crafting narratives with well-defined emotional arcs, brands can cultivate a lasting emotional connection, leaving a profound impact on consumers and reinforcing brand loyalty.

Example: Dove's "Real Beauty" campaign takes consumers through a journey of self-acceptance, leading to cathartic moments of empowerment.

The Role of Storytelling in Shaping Brand Perception: Storytelling plays a pivotal role in shaping how consumers perceive and relate to a brand. Through narratives, brands can control the information they share, framing their identity and values in a way that resonates with their target audience. By crafting compelling stories, brands can establish an emotional connection that goes beyond product features and benefits.

Storytelling influences brand perception by evoking emotions, building authenticity, and reinforcing key messages. One psychological mechanism that underpins this influence is the mirror neuron system, which allows individuals to empathize with the experiences of others. When consumers engage with narratives that feature relatable characters or situations, their mirror neurons activate, fostering a sense of connection and emotional resonance with the brand.

Moreover, storytelling can harness Aristotle's theory of catharsis, a concept derived from ancient Greek drama. Catharsis posits that experiencing strong emotions through stories allows individuals to release and purify their own emotional tensions. In the context of brand storytelling, this theory suggests that narratives that lead to emotional catharsis can leave consumers feeling emotionally satisfied and more positively disposed towards the brand.

Narratives that reflect the brand's history, values, or customer experiences enhance authenticity and build trust. Emotional narratives can trigger feelings of empathy, nostalgia, or aspiration, creating a lasting impression in consumers' minds. Furthermore, stories that embody the hero's journey, overcoming challenges and evolving, resonate with consumers' desire for personal growth and transformation.

In shaping brand perception, consistency is crucial. Brands must ensure that their narratives align with their visual identity, communication style, and overall brand strategy. Effective storytelling can lead to positive associations, loyalty, and advocacy, making it an indispensable tool for brands aiming to create a distinct and resonant brand image in the minds of consumers.

Example: Patagonia's commitment to sustainability is reinforced through stories of environmental activism, enhancing its brand perception.

Crafting Compelling Brand Narratives

Crafting compelling brand narratives is an essential art in today's marketing landscape. Brands that master this skill can create stories that captivate their audience, communicate their values, and establish a strong emotional connection. By strategically structuring narratives and weaving them into their brand identity, companies can foster engagement, loyalty, and a deeper understanding of their products or services. In this section, we delve into the elements and techniques of creating narratives that resonate, exploring how brands can use storytelling to leave a lasting impact on consumers.

Story Structure: Introduction, Conflict, Climax, Resolution: The foundation of a compelling brand narrative lies in its structure. Just as in classic storytelling, a brand narrative follows a well-defined sequence: introduction, conflict, climax, and resolution. The introduction sets the stage, introducing characters, settings, and the initial situation. The conflict introduces challenges or obstacles that the protagonist (brand) must overcome. The climax marks the peak of tension and excitement, where the conflict reaches its highest point. Finally, the resolution brings closure, showing how the conflict is resolved and revealing the outcomes.

Applying this narrative structure to branding allows brands to create stories that engage and resonate with audiences. By identifying relatable challenges or desires that their target audience faces, brands can craft narratives that evoke emotional responses and connections. The resolution provides a sense of closure, allowing consumers to perceive the brand as a solution provider. Successful brands master this storytelling structure to not only convey their message effectively but also to establish a lasting connection with their customers.

Example: McDonald's "McFlurry" ad follows a story structure by introducing a character's craving, leading to the resolution of enjoying a McFlurry.

Hero's Journey Framework and Brand Transformation: The Hero's Journey, a narrative structure coined by Joseph Campbell, has been widely used in literature and storytelling. This framework involves a protagonist (hero) embarking on a transformative journey that involves challenges, growth, and ultimately, a return with newfound wisdom. In the context of branding, the Hero's Journey framework is employed to create narratives that resonate with consumers on a deep level.

Brands can position themselves as the hero, taking customers on a journey of transformation. This transformation might involve overcoming obstacles, facing challenges, and ultimately achieving personal growth or self-discovery. By aligning their brand with the Hero's Journey, companies tap into the universal appeal of storytelling and the innate human desire for progress and change.

Example: Apple's iconic "1984" Super Bowl ad follows the Hero's Journey, positioning the Macintosh as a revolutionary product.

Storytelling Elements: Characters, Settings, and Plot: Characters play a central role in brand narratives. They are the vehicles through which consumers can connect emotionally with the story. Brands often create relatable characters that embody the values and aspirations of their audience. These characters may undergo transformation and growth throughout the narrative, reflecting the brand's own evolution or the desired outcome for customers.

Settings provide the backdrop for the story, creating context and atmosphere. A well-defined setting helps transport consumers into the brand's world, enhancing their emotional engagement. Whether it's a vibrant urban landscape, a serene natural environment, or a futuristic realm, the setting contributes to the emotional resonance of the story.

The plot outlines the sequence of events that unfold in the narrative. It involves challenges, conflicts, and resolutions that keep consumers engaged and invested. Brands leverage plot dynamics to create suspense, curiosity, and emotional highs and lows that mirror the customer journey or the brand's mission.

Example: Guinness's "Surfer" ad showcases a character's journey through rough waters, connecting with the brand's resilient identity.

Developing a Brand's Origin Story for Authenticity: An authentic origin story resonates with consumers by humanizing the brand and showcasing its genuine beginnings. By sharing the challenges, inspirations, and pivotal moments that shaped the brand, companies create a relatable and trustworthy image. This narrative approach taps into consumers' emotional responses, fostering a sense of shared experience and loyalty.

Example: Coca-Cola's origin story of pharmacist John Pemberton's creation reinforces the brand's legacy and authenticity.

Evoking Psychological States Through Stories

In the realm of brand communication, stories have the remarkable ability to evoke a wide spectrum of psychological states in consumers. These emotional states, ranging from happiness and sadness to fear and joy, play a pivotal role in shaping consumer perceptions and decisions. Understanding how narratives influence these psychological states is crucial for brands aiming to establish deeper connections and resonate with their target audience. This section delves into the intricate ways in which storytelling can leverage affective states to create a profound impact on consumer emotions and brand engagement.

Leveraging Affective States: Happiness, Sadness, Fear, Joy: Harnessing the power of emotions, brands strategically use storytelling to invoke specific affective states within consumers. The narrative experience can lead individuals on an emotional journey, from eliciting happiness and joy to evoking sadness and fear. By skillfully tapping into these emotional wellsprings, brands can establish strong emotional connections with their audience. Through the artful manipulation of affective states, storytelling becomes a tool not only for conveying brand messages but also for eliciting profound emotional responses that leave a lasting imprint on consumer perception and behaviour.

Example: Always' "Like a Girl" campaign triggers feelings of empowerment and challenges gender stereotypes, fostering positive emotions.

Narratives and their Impact on Consumer Mood: The narratives presented by brands possess the remarkable ability to influence and modulate consumer moods. Whether through evocative storytelling, relatable characters, or engaging plot twists, brands can shape the emotional trajectory of their audience. Positive, uplifting stories can uplift moods, while tales of challenges and triumphs can create emotional resonance. On the flip side, negative narratives might lead to emotional discomfort. Brands adept at crafting narratives that align with desired consumer moods can effectively influence perceptions, attitudes, and behaviours. The emotional journey triggered by these narratives can become a pivotal factor in how consumers connect with and remember brands, ultimately influencing their decision-making processes.

Example: IKEA's "The Wonderful Everyday" campaign creates a cheerful and uplifting mood by depicting relatable home situations.

Mood Congruency and its Role in Brand Recall: This psychological phenomenon suggests that people tend to remember information better when it aligns with their current emotional state. In the context of branding, this means that if a brand's narrative evokes a particular emotion that resonates with the consumer's current mood, the brand and its message are more likely to be retained in memory. By understanding mood congruency, brands can strategically craft narratives that align with their target audience's emotions.

Example: Cadbury's "Joyville" campaign aligns with feelings of happiness, increasing the likelihood of positive brand recall.

Nostalgia as a Storytelling Tool for Brand Identity:
Nostalgia is a powerful emotional trigger that brands can leverage to create a deep and lasting connection with consumers. By tapping into cherished memories and experiences from the past, brands can evoke feelings of warmth, comfort, and familiarity. Incorporating nostalgic elements in brand narratives allows consumers to relive positive moments, fostering a sense of nostalgia-driven affinity for the brand. When done authentically, nostalgia-driven storytelling not only strengthens brand identity but also facilitates a bridge between the past and present, influencing consumers' present choices and future loyalty.

Example: Coca-Cola's "Share a Coke" campaign taps into nostalgia by featuring personal names on its bottles, evoking fond memories.

Storytelling Across Different Media Platforms

As technology continues to evolve, the art of storytelling has adapted to find resonance across diverse media platforms. From traditional print to digital realms, brands have harnessed the power of storytelling to create immersive experiences that captivate audiences across various touchpoints. This section explores how cross-platform storytelling maintains consistency while adapting to the unique characteristics of each medium. It delves into the world of transmedia narratives, where brand stories can unfold seamlessly across multiple channels, and examines the compelling role of video marketing, podcasts, blogs, and interactive content in brand communication. By leveraging the strengths of different media, brands can cultivate deeper connections and engagement, enhancing the impact of their narrative strategies.

Cross-Platform Storytelling: Consistency and Adaptation: In the rapidly evolving realm of modern communication, brands encounter the challenge of effectively engaging audiences across various platforms. Achieving cross-platform storytelling prowess necessitates a careful equilibrium between maintaining narrative uniformity and tailoring content to suit the distinctive characteristics of each channel. Competent brands strike this balance by upholding the core storyline's coherence and recognizability, regardless of the medium employed— whether social media, websites, or other communication avenues. The preservation of consistency establishes and fortifies brand identity and trust, while the adaptation of content ensures optimal resonance and engagement. This segment delves into the strategies employed by successful brands to seamlessly translate their narratives across diverse platforms, accentuating methods that respect each platform's unique attributes while offering a consistent brand experience.

Example: Nike's "Dream Crazier" campaign uses a consistent message of empowerment across TV ads, social media, and website content.

Transmedia Narratives and Immersive Brand Experiences: Transmedia storytelling enables brands to craft multi-dimensional narratives that span various media channels, creating a more immersive and engaging experience for their audience. This approach allows brands to leverage the strengths of different platforms to convey different facets of their story, creating a more comprehensive and captivating brand universe. Immersive brand experiences are cultivated through these transmedia narratives, fostering deeper connections and interactions with consumers.

Whether it's a combination of videos, articles, interactive content, or virtual reality experiences, transmedia narratives have the power to transform brand communication into an interconnected, engaging journey that captures and sustains consumer interest. This section explores the strategies and tactics employed by brands to create transmedia narratives that elevate brand engagement and foster immersive experiences.

Example: Marvel's cinematic universe spans movies, TV shows, and comics, providing a rich transmedia experience for fans.

Storytelling in Video Marketing: From Commercials to Webisodes:

Video marketing has become a cornerstone of brand communication, offering a dynamic platform to tell compelling stories. Brands utilize videos ranging from concise commercials to longer-form webisodes to convey their narratives. These visual narratives captivate audiences through a combination of audio-visual elements, allowing brands to evoke emotions, convey messages, and establish a distinct brand identity. Whether it's a 30-second teaser or a series of webisodes, video storytelling offers an opportunity to create memorable and impactful brand experiences. This section delves into the art of storytelling within the realm of video marketing, examining how brands leverage the power of moving images to communicate their essence and connect with audiences.

Example: Red Bull's "Stratos" campaign includes a series of videos documenting Felix Baumgartner's historic space jump, creating a captivating narrative.

Podcasts, Blogs, and Interactive Storytelling in Branding: As digital platforms continue to diversify, brands are finding innovative ways to engage audiences through podcasts, blogs, and interactive storytelling. Podcasts offer a unique auditory experience, enabling brands to convey narratives through engaging conversations, interviews, and discussions. Blogs, on the other hand, provide a written avenue for storytelling, allowing brands to share in-depth insights, experiences, and expertise. Interactive storytelling, with its blend of multimedia elements, invites audiences to actively participate in the narrative, forging deeper connections. These mediums empower brands to reach audiences in personalized and interactive ways, enhancing brand engagement and fostering a sense of community. This section explores how podcasts, blogs, and interactive storytelling shape brand narratives and establish meaningful connections with consumers.

Example: Patagonia's podcast "The Dirtbag Diaries," tells stories of outdoor adventures, aligning with the brand's ethos.

Psychological Theories Underpinning Brand Stories

Psychological theories play a pivotal role in understanding the mechanisms behind the impact of brand stories on consumer behaviour and perception. This section delves into the application of several key psychological theories that underpin the effectiveness of brand narratives.

Cognitive Dissonance and its Role in Story Resolution

Cognitive dissonance theory, proposed by Leon Festinger, asserts that individuals experience discomfort when they hold conflicting beliefs or attitudes. In the context of brand storytelling, cognitive dissonance can be employed to create tension within a narrative. By presenting characters or situations that face conflicting choices or values, brands can immerse audiences in a compelling story. As the narrative unfolds, the resolution of cognitive dissonance offers a sense of closure and satisfaction to audiences, resulting in a more impactful and memorable brand experience. For instance, a brand might introduce a character torn between loyalty to their values and the allure of a new opportunity. The eventual resolution of this conflict within the story not only keeps the audience engaged but also resonates with their own experiences of resolving inner conflicts.

Example: Volkswagen's "The Force" commercial creates dissonance by depicting a child using the Force, which is then resolved humorously.

Social Identity Theory and Story-Induced Group Affiliation

Social identity theory, developed by Henri Tajfel, emphasizes how individuals derive a sense of self and belonging from the groups they identify with. In the context of brand stories, this theory highlights the importance of creating narratives that resonate with specific group identities. Brands can craft narratives that tap into cultural, social, or subcultural affiliations, allowing consumers to see themselves as part of a larger community that shares common values and aspirations. For example, a sportswear brand may tell a story of determination and perseverance, drawing on the narrative of athletes who overcome challenges. By aligning with the target audience's aspirations for self-improvement and belonging to a community of achievers, the brand fosters a deeper connection.

Example: Nike's "Just Do It" campaign encourages individuals to identify with a community of athletes, creating a shared identity.

Psychological Ownership and Attachment through Stories

Psychological ownership refers to the sense of control and connection individuals feel towards an object, idea, or entity. Brand stories can leverage this concept by creating narratives that allow consumers to emotionally invest in the brand's journey. Through relatable characters and relatable challenges, brands can encourage consumers to develop a sense of ownership over the brand's successes and transformations. For instance, a tech company might narrate its evolution from a humble start-up to a global powerhouse, allowing consumers to feel a sense of pride and attachment to the brand's growth.

Example: Apple's narrative of innovation and creativity fosters a sense of ownership and loyalty among its customers.

Applying Theories of Persuasion to Narrative Branding

Theories of persuasion, such as the elaboration likelihood model and the peripheral route to persuasion, offer insights into how narratives can influence consumer attitudes and behaviours. By strategically integrating persuasive elements into brand narratives, marketers can guide audiences towards desired outcomes. Brands can use stories to appeal to consumers' emotions and values, fostering a stronger connection. For instance, a charity organization might tell a story of an individual's transformative journey from adversity to success, invoking emotions of empathy and compassion to encourage donations.

Example: TOMS Shoes' One for One campaign appeals to consumers' sense of social responsibility, leveraging persuasion principles.

Storytelling Ethics and Authenticity

Storytelling in branding raises important ethical considerations, particularly in maintaining authenticity and transparency. Brands must navigate the fine line between crafting engaging narratives and misrepresenting their identity or values. Ethical consumerism, a concept emphasizing responsible consumption aligned with personal values, plays a pivotal role in shaping consumers' perceptions of brands.

Ethical Consumerism and Cultural Appropriation

Brands that embrace ethical consumerism often align their narratives with social and environmental values, aiming to build genuine connections with conscious consumers. For instance, Patagonia, an outdoor apparel company, is known for its commitment to environmental sustainability. The brand's narrative weaves stories about conservation efforts, promoting transparency in their supply chain, and encouraging consumers to make ethical choices in their purchasing decisions.

However, cultural appropriation can arise when brands adopt elements of a culture without proper understanding or respect, potentially leading to offense or misrepresentation. An example is the use of indigenous symbols or practices for commercial purposes. When Victoria's Secret featured a model wearing a Native American headdress during a fashion show, it sparked controversy for appropriating sacred symbols. This instance demonstrated the importance of cultural sensitivity and authenticity in storytelling.

In a landscape where consumers value authenticity and ethical practices, brands must carefully craft narratives that reflect their values and resonate with their target audience. Balancing the art of storytelling with ethical considerations ensures that brands maintain trust and build lasting relationships with their customers.

Personalization and User-Generated Brand Stories

Personalization and user-generated brand stories are dynamic strategies that empower consumers to play a pivotal role in shaping brand narratives. By intertwining individual experiences and contributions, brands forge potent connections that extend beyond transactional interactions. Personal brand narratives, exemplified by Nike's "Just Do It" campaign, enable consumers to share their personal journeys of overcoming challenges, aligning their achievements with the brand's ethos. Simultaneously, user-generated content initiatives like Starbucks' White Cup Contest foster a collective sense of creativity and camaraderie, transforming customers into co-creators of the brand's visual identity. Moreover, the craft of personalized brand narratives, demonstrated by Coca-Cola's "Share a Coke" campaign, utilizes data insights to tailor messages to individual preferences, generating an intrinsic link between consumers and the brand. These practices are exemplified in Airbnb's humanizing depiction of hosts' stories, GoPro's vibrant user-generated content network, and Coca-Cola's customization efforts, collectively illustrating the potential of these strategies to imbue narratives with authenticity, community, and personal resonance, thereby cultivating enduring brand loyalty and engagement.

Measuring the Impact of Brand Narratives

Measuring the impact of brand narratives involves a multi-faceted approach. Neuro metrics, as employed by Coca-Cola in a study, delve into brain activity to gauge emotional engagement, revealing how narratives evoke neural responses and influence consumer sentiment. Combining quantitative and qualitative methods, Starbucks assessed the effects of its "Race Together" campaign, analysing social media mentions, sentiment analysis, and focus groups to comprehend the narrative's resonance. Metrics tracking consumer sharing and virality, such as the ALS Ice Bucket Challenge, demonstrate the expansive reach of narratives, revealing their potential for generating organic brand advocacy. Storytelling analytics, like those employed by Airbnb, involve sentiment analysis and visualization tools to map emotional trajectories, enabling brands to track narrative arcs and tailor their strategies for enhanced resonance. These approaches underscore the vital role of measurement in refining brand narratives, ensuring they resonate effectively and drive desired consumer actions.

Future Trends in Brand Storytelling

The future of brand storytelling embraces cutting-edge technologies and dynamic approaches. Immersive technologies like Virtual Reality (VR) and Augmented Reality (AR), as seen in IKEA's AR app enabling customers to visualize furniture in their homes, redefine consumer engagement through interactive and immersive experiences.

Brands like Netflix employ AI to create personalized, interactive narratives, where viewers dictate storyline outcomes, enhancing engagement and uniqueness. Crowdsourced storytelling, exemplified by Lay's "Do Us a Flavor" campaign, empowers consumers to co-create narratives, fostering a sense of ownership and community. With the evolution of storytelling in an interconnected world, brands such as Coca-Cola use social media platforms to interlink narratives across channels, enhancing audience engagement. AI-driven storytelling, demonstrated by The Washington Post's Heliograf, generates personalized narratives at scale, demonstrating the potential for tailored, data-driven brand stories. These trends illuminate the transformation of brand storytelling, leveraging technology, collaboration, and connectivity to captivate consumers in novel and engaging ways.

Cross-Cultural Narratives and Cultural Psychology

Cross-cultural narratives intersect with cultural psychology to create compelling brand stories that resonate across diverse audiences. Recognizing cross-cultural story universals, brands like McDonald's adapt their messaging while retaining core values, bridging cultural gaps through universally relatable themes. Embracing cultural relativism and adaptation, Airbnb's "A Different Paris" campaign tailors stories to local customs, fostering authenticity and resonating with global audiences. Cultural influences on story perception and emotional resonance are evident in Dove's "Real Beauty" campaign, addressing diverse beauty ideals, generating emotional connections, and promoting inclusivity. Brands avoid cultural stereotypes and prioritize sensitivity, as demonstrated by Pepsi's controversial ad, which misjudged cultural nuances and sparked backlash. This underscores the importance of culturally aware storytelling, exemplified by Disney's Moana, celebrating Polynesian culture with authenticity and respect. In a globalized world, cross-cultural narratives, when thoughtfully crafted, transcend boundaries and foster deep emotional connections while avoiding pitfalls of cultural insensitivity.

Neuroaesthetics and Visual Storytelling

Neuroaesthetics combines with visual storytelling to enhance brand communication through captivating visuals. Understanding the neuroscience of visual appeal, brands like Apple integrate minimalist design principles to evoke a sense of elegance and sophistication, aligning with consumers' aesthetic preferences. Visual storytelling elements such as composition, imagery, and flow are expertly employed by Nike's "Just Do It" campaign, utilizing dynamic visuals to convey determination and empowerment, resonating with audiences worldwide. The power of visual metaphors is exemplified by Coca-Cola's "Hilltop" ad, where diverse individuals unite over shared values, employing imagery to evoke emotions and tell a powerful story. Brands like Airbnb harness visual storytelling to highlight unique accommodations, making travel experiences vivid and relatable. Incorporating visual storytelling in brand identity design is evident in Starbucks' iconic logo, which visually encapsulates the brand's promise of warmth and community, creating an instantly recognizable symbol. Leveraging neuroaesthetics and visual storytelling enables brands to evoke emotions, foster connections, and establish enduring identities in consumers' minds.

NEUROMARKETING RESEARCH METHODS

Neuromarketing employs diverse methodologies to uncover consumer insights while considering ethical considerations. Combining neuroimaging and behavioural metrics, Frito-Lay conducted a study assessing consumer preferences by measuring brain activity and purchase intent simultaneously. Eye-tracking studies, exemplified by Tobii's work, reveal visual attention patterns guiding packaging design optimization. Implicit Association Tests (IAT) expose unconscious brand perceptions, as seen with a study by Coca-Cola, revealing associations between the brand and positive emotions. Measuring emotional responses through facial expressions, Mars used Emotiv's EEG headsets to gauge consumers' emotional engagement with their products. Neuroaesthetics and design evaluation underpin BMW's testing of design elements, gauging consumers' neural responses to refine visual appeal. Neuromarketing field studies, such as Pepsico's research, bring ecological validity, understanding consumers' real-world interactions. Neuromarketing in virtual environments, showcased by Oculus and its collaboration with Samsung, enables brands to evaluate user experiences in simulated scenarios. These methods intertwine ethics and innovation to offer deeper insights into consumer behaviour and shape effective marketing strategies.

Ethical Considerations in Neuromarketing Research

Ethics are paramount in neuromarketing research, with informed consent and participant rights taking precedence. For instance, Nielsen Neuro's collaboration with Reckitt Benckiser ensured participants were well-informed and empowered to withdraw during the study. Deception, though sometimes used for experimental control, must be carefully managed to avoid psychological harm, as seen in PepsiCo's adherence to stringent ethical protocols. Transparency is pivotal; Samsung's partnership with Emotiv showcases the responsible use of neuro insights to improve user experiences, ensuring trust with consumers. Ethical guidelines, exemplified by Neuroethics.ai, govern the sharing and publishing of neuro data to prevent misuse and uphold participant confidentiality, as showcased by Procter & Gamble's commitment to ethical data handling. These considerations align with industry standards, safeguarding both participants and brands while enhancing the credibility and reliability of neuromarketing research.

Combining Neuroimaging and Behavioural Metrics

The integration of neuroimaging and behavioural metrics offers a comprehensive understanding of consumer behaviour. By combining EEG and fMRI data, as demonstrated by NeuroFocus (now Nielsen Neuro) in partnership with CBS, deeper insights into cognitive and emotional responses are gained. Brands like Toyota have correlated brain activity with eye-tracking patterns to unravel how consumers engage with visual stimuli. Multimodal approaches, as seen in Coca-Cola's collaboration with Neurensics, provide a holistic view by merging neuro data with behavioural metrics, yielding enhanced insights. The utilization of big data analysis, exemplified by Google's neuro study on YouTube ads, allows for the interpretation of multi-layered neuro insights, leading to informed marketing strategies. This integration paves the way for a more nuanced understanding of consumer perceptions and responses, ultimately empowering brands to tailor their approaches effectively.

PSYCHOLOGY OF BRANDING

The psychology of branding delves into the intricate realm of consumer perception and connection. It encompasses various facets, including the psychological foundations of brand identity, where brands like Apple evoke emotional loyalty through their innovative and aspirational image. Brand archetypes, as seen with Nike's portrayal of the Hero archetype, resonate deeply with consumers, eliciting powerful psychological impacts. Brands adept at leveraging personality traits, such as Starbucks' friendly and approachable demeanor, forge strong connections. Emotions play a pivotal role in brand attachment, exemplified by Coca-Cola's ability to evoke nostalgic sentiments through its campaigns. Trust is nurtured by brand transparency, as seen in Patagonia's ethical practices. Brands like Harley-Davidson align with consumers' self-concept, evoking a sense of identity. Rituals, as demonstrated by Starbucks' coffee experience, enhance brand engagement. Nostalgia-driven bonds, as with Disney, create profound connections. Community-building by brands like Apple fosters social identity, while triggers like personalized experiences contribute to brand loyalty. Neuromarketing uncovers subconscious influences, while brands like BMW become an extension of consumers' selves, illustrating the concept of symbolic brand ownership. These psychological dimensions intertwine to shape profound consumer-brand relationships.

The Psychological Foundations of Brand Identity

Brand identity is a cornerstone of consumer psychology, encompassing key elements such as logos, names, slogans, and colours that collectively form a distinct brand persona. The development of brand identity involves a meticulous journey from the brand's vision to its perception in consumers' minds, with Apple's iconic logo symbolizing innovation and simplicity. Perceived brand consistency reinforces consumer trust, exemplified by McDonald's consistent branding across its global outlets. Brand identity also serves as a potent tool for differentiation amidst competitors; for instance, Coca-Cola's red and white colour scheme instantly sets it apart. The psychological underpinnings of brand identity resonate through each component, shaping consumers' perceptions, emotions, and loyalty.

Brand Archetypes and Their Psychological Impact

Drawing inspiration from Carl Jung's archetypes, brand archetypes are symbolic representations that tap into universal themes, evoking deep-rooted emotions and associations. Through brand archetype mapping, companies align their personalities with these archetypes to foster emotional resonance with consumers. Nike embodies the Hero archetype, inspiring individuals to overcome challenges, as seen in its empowering "Just Do It" slogan. However, balancing authenticity is vital; Dove's nurturing Mother archetype is exemplified by campaigns promoting real beauty. By understanding and harnessing these archetypes, brands forge stronger connections by resonating with consumers' collective unconscious, nurturing trust and loyalty.

Carl Jung's Archetypes in Branding: Hero, Sage, Lover, and More

Carl Jung's archetypes, which represent universal human themes and behaviours, have been harnessed by brands to establish compelling identities. The Hero archetype, seen in brands like Nike, motivates individuals to conquer challenges and transform their lives. The Sage, as embodied by Google, signifies wisdom and enlightenment. The Lover, epitomized by brands like Victoria's Secret, invokes passion and desire. Each archetype taps into deep-seated psychological patterns, forging connections that resonate with consumers' emotions and aspirations. These archetypes provide a powerful framework for crafting brand narratives and fostering meaningful relationships with customers.

Brand Archetype Mapping: Matching Persona to Target Audience

Brand archetype mapping involves aligning brand personas with specific target audiences based on psychological archetypes. By understanding the traits, values, and desires associated with each archetype, businesses can tailor their messaging to resonate more deeply with their intended consumers. For instance, an Innocent archetype might appeal to families seeking safety and simplicity, while a Rebel archetype could engage a younger audience looking for disruption and rebellion. This strategic alignment enhances brand-consumer connections, fostering authenticity and engagement.

Emotional Resonance Through Archetypal Associations

Creating emotional resonance through archetypal associations involves infusing brands with traits and narratives that align with universal human experiences and values. By tapping into archetypal themes like Heroism, Innocence, or Wisdom, brands can trigger emotional connections that resonate deeply with consumers. For instance, an outdoor apparel brand embodying the Explorer archetype can evoke a sense of adventure and freedom, appealing to those seeking exploration and new experiences. This emotional alignment fosters a strong bond between the brand and its audience, enhancing loyalty and brand preference through shared emotional experiences.

Leveraging Brand Personality for Connection

Leveraging brand personality involves imbuing a brand with human-like traits and characteristics, allowing consumers to connect with it on a personal and emotional level. Brand personality dimensions such as Sincerity, Excitement, Competence, and others shape how consumers perceive and relate to a brand. By crafting a humanized brand personality through communication strategies that embody these traits, brands can foster authentic connections with their audience. This connection goes beyond functional attributes and taps into emotional resonance, leading to the development of a stronger consumer-brand relationship. Consistency in expressing the brand's personality across various touchpoints, from advertising to customer interactions, further reinforces the emotional bond and reinforces the brand's identity in the minds of consumers.

The Role of Emotions in Brand Attachment

Emotions play a pivotal role in fostering strong brand attachment, going beyond rational considerations and tapping into consumers' deeper feelings and experiences. Emotional branding is the process of creating meaningful connections by eliciting specific emotional responses through brand-related stimuli. For instance, Apple's marketing consistently focuses on emotions, invoking a sense of belonging and creativity among its consumers. Emotional contagion refers to the phenomenon where emotions expressed by a brand can influence consumers' emotional states, subsequently impacting their engagement and loyalty. For instance, Coca-Cola's holiday campaigns evoke feelings of joy and togetherness, spreading a positive emotional contagion. The neurological basis of emotional brand attachment lies in the brain's reward system, particularly the release of dopamine during positive emotional experiences with a brand. For example, Starbucks fosters emotional attachment by curating cozy environments that trigger feelings of comfort and relaxation. Employing emotional branding strategies, such as storytelling, personalization, and empathy, can create lasting emotional connections that drive long-term loyalty. Nike's "Just Do It" campaign emotionally resonates with consumers, encouraging them to overcome challenges and embrace a sense of empowerment. Overall, harnessing emotions in branding allows companies to forge deep and enduring relationships with their customers.

Psychological Triggers for Brand Switching

Psychological triggers often drive consumers to consider switching from one brand to another, highlighting the complex interplay of cognitive processes, emotions, and perceptions. Cognitive dissonance emerges when consumers experience a discrepancy between their expectations and actual experiences with a brand, leading to dissatisfaction. For instance, if a customer buys a product expecting high quality but encounters issues, cognitive dissonance may drive them to explore alternatives. Perceived value and satisfaction also play a crucial role in brand switching. When consumers perceive a competitor's offering as providing greater value or satisfaction, they may be motivated to switch. Brands can leverage psychological triggers to prevent defection by enhancing their value proposition and addressing pain points. Apple's commitment to quality and innovative design, combined with a seamless user experience, minimizes the risk of customer defection. However, companies must exercise ethical considerations to prevent consumer coercion. For example, a brand shouldn't manipulate consumer insecurities or fears to discourage switching. Instead, brands can focus on building authentic relationships, addressing concerns transparently, and continually enhancing their offerings. Dove's "Real Beauty" campaign embodies this approach, celebrating diverse body images and fostering a positive self-perception among its consumers. Ultimately, understanding and addressing psychological triggers for brand switching allows brands to proactively retain their customers while maintaining ethical standards.

Neuromarketing and the Subconscious Brand Influence

Neuromarketing delves into the realm of subconscious cognition, aiming to understand and influence consumer behaviour on an unconscious level. Subliminal priming, a technique used in neuromarketing, involves exposing consumers to subtle cues or stimuli that activate specific associations without their conscious awareness. This can significantly impact brand perception. For instance, a study showed that briefly exposing participants to images of luxury items before presenting a brand led them to perceive that brand as more upscale and desirable.

The power of subconscious associations extends to consumer choices. Neuromarketers tap into emotions and memories linked to positive stimuli to create favourable brand associations. Coca-Cola's iconic red and white colours, along with its joyful advertisements, evoke feelings of happiness and enjoyment. These subconscious associations are then reinforced in consumers' minds when making choices.

CONSUMER BEHAVIOUR ANALYSIS IN BRANDING

Consumer Behaviour Analysis in Branding is an in-depth exploration of the intricate interplay between consumers and brands. This chapter delves into the realm of heuristics and their impact on brand choices, uncovering how cognitive shortcuts influence consumers' decision-making processes. It delves into the realms of motivation and emotional triggers, revealing how brands strategically tap into consumers' aspirations and emotions to foster engagement and loyalty. Furthermore, the chapter emphasizes the significance of analysing consumer journeys, shedding light on the intricate paths individuals traverse from awareness to purchase and beyond. It also delves into consumer perception and cognitive biases, elucidating how perceptual filters and biases shape how consumers perceive brands and their offerings. By comprehending these multifaceted dimensions, brands can craft targeted strategies that resonate with consumer behaviour, aspirations, and psychology, fostering lasting brand-consumer relationships.

Decision-Making Heuristics and Brand Choices

Decision-Making Heuristics and Brand Choices explores the cognitive shortcuts that consumers employ when making decisions, illustrating how these mental shortcuts influence their brand preferences and choices. By understanding these heuristic strategies, brands can tailor their messaging and positioning to align with consumers' intuitive decision-making processes, thus enhancing their appeal and fostering favourable brand choices.

Example: Coca-Cola's Availability Heuristic - Through consistent and pervasive advertising, Coca-Cola ensures its brand is easily accessible and visible in various contexts, from vending machines to commercials. This availability, coupled with the brand's iconic red and white colours, triggers consumers' heuristic thinking, making Coca-Cola a top-of-mind choice when they think of carbonated beverages.

Motivations and Emotional Triggers in Consumer Behaviour

Consumers are driven by various motivations and emotional triggers that influence their brand preferences and purchase decisions. Motivations can be intrinsic, such as personal satisfaction, or extrinsic, like social recognition. Emotional triggers, like joy, fear, or nostalgia, evoke powerful responses that impact brand resonance. For instance, the luxury brand Chanel effectively taps into consumers' desire for exclusivity and status, using emotional triggers like sophistication and elegance to establish a strong emotional connection. By aligning their marketing strategies with consumers' motivations and emotional triggers, brands can create compelling narratives and experiences that resonate on a deeper level, fostering loyalty and engagement.

Example - Nike - "Just Do it" Campaign

Analysing Consumer Journeys and Touchpoints

Analysing consumer journeys and touchpoints involves understanding the various stages a consumer goes through when interacting with a brand and identifying the key points of contact or touchpoints during this journey. This process helps brands gain insights into consumer behaviour, preferences, and pain points, enabling them to optimize the overall brand experience. For example, a company like Starbucks carefully analyses its consumer journey from the moment a customer enters the store to the point of making a purchase and beyond. By mapping out these touchpoints and understanding the emotions and behaviours associated with each stage, Starbucks can tailor its offerings, store layout, and customer service to create a seamless and satisfying experience, ultimately enhancing customer loyalty and brand perception.

- **Customer Journey Mapping: Visualizing the Consumer Experience**

Customer journey mapping involves visually illustrating the entire experience a customer has with a brand, from the initial contact to the final interaction. It helps businesses identify pain points, optimize touchpoints, and enhance overall customer satisfaction.

Example: Starbucks - They use customer journey mapping to enhance its in-store experience and digital interactions.

- **Touchpoints and Micro-Moments in Brand Interactions**

Touchpoints and micro-moments are critical moments of interaction between consumers and brands, such as when consumers search for information or make quick decisions. An example is Nike's mobile app, which provides personalized content and shopping options, enhancing the brand's connection with consumers during their fitness journeys.

- **Emotional Milestones and Key Decision Points in Journeys**

Emotional milestones and key decision points in consumer journeys are pivotal moments that influence brand perceptions. Apple's product launch events, like the unveiling of new iPhones, evoke excitement and anticipation among consumers, strengthening their emotional connection with the brand.

- **Optimizing Consumer Journeys for Seamless Brand Experiences**

Optimizing consumer journeys ensures seamless brand experiences. Amazon's one-click ordering process simplifies online shopping, enhancing user convenience and aligning with their customer-centric approach.

Consumer Perception and Cognitive Biases in Branding

Consumer Perception and Cognitive Biases play a pivotal role in shaping brand interactions and decisions. In the world of branding, understanding how individuals perceive and interpret information is essential for crafting effective strategies that resonate with target audiences. The way consumers perceive brands, products, and messages is influenced by cognitive biases, which are systematic patterns of thinking that can lead to deviations from rational judgment. This section delves into the intricate relationship between consumer perception and cognitive biases, highlighting how these psychological mechanisms can impact brand positioning, messaging, and overall consumer behaviour. Through exploration of various cognitive biases and their implications, this section unveils the complexities of consumer decision-making processes in the context of branding.

- **Perceptual Mapping: How Consumers Mentally Position Brands**

Perceptual Mapping visually represents how consumers mentally position brands in relation to each other based on perceived attributes. An example is how Apple's branding is associated with innovation and sleek design, illustrating how perceptual mapping aids in understanding consumer perceptions and competitive positioning.

- **Cognitive Biases in Perceived Quality and Value Assessment**

Cognitive biases influence consumers' assessment of quality and value. For instance, the "anchoring bias" can impact how consumers perceive the value of a product based on its initial price. A live example is IKEA's use of "asymmetric dominance" by offering a higher-priced item next to a similar but pricier alternative, influencing perceived value and choice.

- **Halo Effect and its Impact on Brand Perception**

The halo effect leads consumers to generalize positive perceptions of a brand to its other attributes. Apple's strong brand image, for instance, positively influences perceptions of its product quality, even if not directly related.

- **Addressing Confirmation Bias in Brand Evaluation**

Confirmation bias, a tendency to favour information confirming pre-existing beliefs, can lead consumers to overlook a brand's shortcomings. A live example is Tesla, where fans might downplay recalls due to their positive perception of the brand's innovative image.

Brand Attitudes and Cognitive Dissonance

The focus is on the intricate relationship between consumers' attitudes towards brands and the cognitive dissonance that may arise when those attitudes clash with their behaviours or external influences. Consumers form brand attitudes based on their perceptions, emotions, and experiences, which can lead to brand loyalty or preference. However, when inconsistencies arise between their attitudes and actions, cognitive dissonance emerges, creating discomfort that prompts them to seek resolution. Brands often work to address this dissonance through effective communication, customer service, and aligning brand messages with consumers' actual experiences. Live brand examples, such as Apple's loyal customer base despite occasional product issues, illustrate how attitudes can mitigate cognitive dissonance and maintain brand allegiance.

- **Cognitive Consistency and Attitude-Behaviour Alignment**

Cognitive Consistency refers to the psychological preference for individuals to maintain harmony between their beliefs, attitudes, and behaviours. Attitude-Behaviour Alignment is the congruence between one's attitudes and their actual actions.

- **Elaboration Likelihood Model: Central and Peripheral Routes to Persuasion**

The Elaboration Likelihood Model proposes two routes to persuasion: the Central Route, where people carefully consider information, and the Peripheral Route, where cues like visuals influence decision-making.

Example: Coca-Cola employs the peripheral route by using engaging and emotionally appealing advertisements to influence consumer attitudes, particularly during festive seasons.

- **Cognitive Dissonance in Brand Switching and Post-Purchase Regret**

Cognitive dissonance in brand switching occurs when a consumer feels discomfort after changing brands, as their choice challenges their initial beliefs. Post-purchase regret involves a sense of unease following a purchase, seen when a consumer questions their decision.

Example: After switching to **Apple iPhone** from a competitor, a consumer might experience cognitive dissonance due to the higher cost, leading to potential post-purchase regret.

- **Persuasion Strategies for Resolving Cognitive Dissonance**

Persuasion strategies for resolving cognitive dissonance involve using communication to align consumer beliefs with their actions, often by emphasizing positive aspects of the chosen option.

Example: Patagonia employs persuasion by highlighting its sustainable practices, reducing consumer dissonance for paying higher prices for eco-friendly clothing.

Brand Attitudes and Cognitive Dissonance

The focus is on the intricate relationship between consumers' attitudes towards brands and the cognitive dissonance that may arise when those attitudes clash with their behaviours or external influences. Consumers form brand attitudes based on their perceptions, emotions, and experiences, which can lead to brand loyalty or preference. However, when inconsistencies arise between their attitudes and actions, cognitive dissonance emerges, creating discomfort that prompts them to seek resolution. Brands often work to address this dissonance through effective communication, customer service, and aligning brand messages with consumers' actual experiences. Live brand examples, such as Apple's loyal customer base despite occasional product issues, illustrate how attitudes can mitigate cognitive dissonance and maintain brand allegiance.

- **Cognitive Consistency and Attitude-Behaviour Alignment**

Cognitive Consistency refers to the psychological preference for individuals to maintain harmony between their beliefs, attitudes, and behaviours. Attitude-Behaviour Alignment is the congruence between one's attitudes and their actual actions.

- **Elaboration Likelihood Model: Central and Peripheral Routes to Persuasion**

The Elaboration Likelihood Model proposes two routes to persuasion: the Central Route, where people carefully consider information, and the Peripheral Route, where cues like visuals influence decision-making.

Example: **Coca-Cola** employs the peripheral route by using engaging and emotionally appealing advertisements to influence consumer attitudes, particularly during festive seasons.

- **Cognitive Dissonance in Brand Switching and Post-Purchase Regret**

Cognitive dissonance in brand switching occurs when a consumer feels discomfort after changing brands, as their choice challenges their initial beliefs. Post-purchase regret involves a sense of unease following a purchase, seen when a consumer questions their decision.

Example: After switching to **Apple iPhone** from a competitor, a consumer might experience cognitive dissonance due to the higher cost, leading to potential post-purchase regret.

- **Persuasion Strategies for Resolving Cognitive Dissonance**

Persuasion strategies for resolving cognitive dissonance involve using communication to align consumer beliefs with their actions, often by emphasizing positive aspects of the chosen option.

Example: Patagonia employs persuasion by highlighting its sustainable practices, reducing consumer dissonance for paying higher prices for eco-friendly clothing.

Social Influence and Group Dynamics in Brand Choices

Social influence and group dynamics heavily influence brand choices, as individuals often conform to the preferences of their social circles and reference groups. People tend to align their brand decisions with those around them, and brands capitalize on this by creating identities that resonate with specific communities. This fosters a sense of belonging and shared values, shaping consumer preferences and driving brand loyalty.

- **Social Proof: Leveraging Others' Behaviour as a Cue**

Social proof involves using the behaviour and choices of others as a cue for decision-making. Brands often leverage this psychological phenomenon by showcasing testimonials, reviews, or user-generated content to influence consumers.

Example: Airbnb effectively employs social proof by displaying reviews and ratings from previous guests, influencing potential customers' decisions and building trust in the booking process.

- **Reference Groups and Aspirational Brand Associations**

Reference groups are the social circles individuals compare themselves to, influencing their attitudes and choices. Brands create aspirational associations by linking their products with desirable reference groups, appealing to consumers' aspirations and identity.

Example: Rolex utilizes aspirational brand associations by positioning their watches as symbols of success and luxury, appealing to consumers who aspire to be part of an exclusive and high-status reference group.

- **Opinion Leaders and their Role in Shaping Brand Preferences**

Opinion leaders are individuals with significant influence over others' beliefs and choices. Brands strategically engage these figures to shape brand preferences by leveraging their credibility and reach.

Example: Oprah Winfrey as an opinion leader has shaped brand preferences by endorsing products on her platform, impacting consumer choices through her credibility and broad audience reach.

- **Identifying and Targeting Opinion Leaders in Brand Campaigns**

Identifying and targeting opinion leaders involves recognizing individuals who sway others' opinions and tailoring brand campaigns to gain their endorsement. Brands often collaborate with these influencers to enhance credibility and expand their reach.

Example: Nike effectively employs this strategy by partnering with athletes like **LeBron James**, capitalizing on his influence to promote their products, resonating with sports enthusiasts and driving brand engagement.

Brand Loyalty and Habitual Buying Behaviour

Brand loyalty refers to consumers' strong preference for a specific brand, often due to positive experiences, emotional connections, and consistent quality. Habitual buying behaviour involves repetitive purchasing of a particular brand out of routine or convenience, driven by established patterns and familiarity. Both concepts contribute to a brand's sustained success and customer retention.

- **The Loyalty Loop: From Brand Awareness to Advocacy**

The Loyalty Loop illustrates the journey customers take from brand awareness to becoming loyal advocates. Brands foster this cycle by delivering exceptional experiences that turn customers into promoters, as seen with **Starbucks**, where customers not only purchase coffee but also proudly share their Starbucks experiences, contributing to ongoing brand advocacy and loyalty.

- ## Habit Formation and the Role of Cue-Routine-Reward

Habit formation involves the automatic response to cues with specific routines that lead to rewards. Brands leverage this by creating consistent cues and rewards, as seen with **Instagram**, where users are prompted by notifications (cue) to check the app, scrolling through posts (routine), resulting in social interaction and content discovery (reward), reinforcing the habit loop.

- ## Maintaining Brand Loyalty through Reinforcement

Maintaining brand loyalty involves reinforcing positive experiences and associations to encourage repeat purchases. **Amazon Prime** exemplifies this by offering exclusive benefits like fast shipping and streaming, reinforcing loyalty through ongoing rewards and services that enhance the overall customer experience.

- ## Overcoming Inertia: Strategies to Break Habitual Patterns

Overcoming inertia entails using strategies to disrupt habitual buying behaviours and encourage consumers to consider alternatives. **Uber** effectively does this by introducing limited-time promotions or discounts, prompting riders to reevaluate their transportation choices and potentially switch from their habitual patterns to try out the new offerings.

Behavioural Economics and Brand Decision-Making

Behavioural economics examines how psychological and emotional factors influence the choices individuals make, shedding light on the complexities of decision-making beyond traditional rational models. In the realm of brand decision-making, this interdisciplinary field explores the cognitive biases, heuristics, and emotional triggers that steer consumers toward certain brands and products. By delving into the nuances of human behaviour, behavioural economics offers insights into why individuals often deviate from purely rational decisions, illuminating the pivotal role of emotions, social influences, and mental shortcuts in shaping brand preferences. Understanding these dynamics is crucial for brands seeking to create impactful marketing strategies and cultivate enduring relationships with consumers in today's intricate and ever-evolving marketplace.

- **Prospect Theory and the Psychology of Risk Perception**

Prospect Theory explores how people evaluate potential outcomes, emphasizing that individuals are more sensitive to potential losses than gains. **Apple** leverages this by offering extended warranties and insurance options at the point of purchase, addressing consumers' risk aversion and enhancing their sense of security, which ultimately influences brand trust and loyalty.

- **Endowment Effect and the Valuation of Brands**

The Endowment Effect is the tendency to assign higher value to items simply because one owns them. **Nike** capitalizes on this by creating limited-edition sneakers, triggering consumers' perception of exclusivity and ownership, which drives up the perceived value of the brand and its products, influencing purchasing decisions and brand loyalty.

- **Anchoring and Default Bias in Brand Pricing**

Anchoring is the cognitive bias where initial information (the "anchor") influences subsequent decisions. Brands like **Tesla** employ this by presenting a higher-priced version of their electric cars first, anchoring consumers' expectations, which can lead to a perceived value in choosing a slightly less expensive option, effectively guiding consumers towards desired purchasing decisions.

- **Designing Choice Architecture for Optimal Brand Decision-Making**

Designing choice architecture involves structuring the way options are presented to guide consumers toward preferred decisions. **Netflix** exemplifies this by using personalized recommendations and auto-play features, influencing viewers to continue watching content aligned with their preferences, ultimately enhancing the user experience and driving engagement with the platform.

Neuromarketing Insights into Consumer Behaviour

Neuromarketing offers valuable insights into consumer behaviour by tapping into the neurological and psychological processes underlying decision-making. Through techniques like brain imaging and biometric measurements, it reveals how individuals respond to marketing stimuli, uncovering subconscious emotions, preferences, and attention patterns that traditional methods might miss. By understanding the brain's intricate reactions to branding, pricing, and product presentation, businesses gain a deeper comprehension of what truly resonates with consumers, allowing for more targeted and effective strategies that enhance engagement, loyalty, and overall brand success.

- **Neuro Insights into Subconscious Consumer Reactions**

Neuro insights unveil subconscious consumer reactions by studying brain activity and physiological responses to marketing stimuli. **Coca-Cola** used EEG scans to assess brain responses, revealing how their packaging designs trigger positive emotions, thus enabling the brand to refine packaging to elicit more favourable subconscious reactions and drive consumer preference.

- **The Neurological Basis of Brand Preferences**

The neurological basis of brand preferences lies in how the brain processes emotions, memories, and associations tied to specific brands, influencing consumer choices. **Disney** strategically crafts enchanting experiences that trigger positive emotions and vivid memories, forming strong neural connections that establish enduring brand loyalty among both children and adults.

- **Neuromarketing and Predictive Consumer Behaviour Modeling**

Neuromarketing informs predictive consumer behaviour modeling by analysing brain responses to stimuli, enabling businesses to anticipate consumer choices more accurately. **Amazon** utilizes browsing and purchase history data combined with neuromarketing insights to develop personalized product recommendations, enhancing the online shopping experience and increasing the likelihood of future purchases based on consumers' subconscious preferences.

- **Applying Neuro Insights for Ethical and Effective Brand Communication**

Applying neuro insights in brand communication involves leveraging a deep understanding of cognitive processes to create ethical and impactful messaging. **Dove** successfully employs this by using emotionally resonant storytelling and relatable visuals in their campaigns, aligning with consumers' neural responses to authenticity and promoting positive body image, thus fostering trust and long-term brand loyalty.

CLUSTER/PATTERN ANALYSIS FROM A BRAND PSYCHOLOGY PERSPECTIVE

Cluster or pattern analysis, from a brand psychology perspective, refers to a powerful analytical approach that identifies and groups distinct behavioural and attitudinal patterns among consumers. This method delves into the intricate connections between consumer actions, preferences, and psychological factors, revealing nuanced segments within a brand's target audience. By dissecting these clusters, brands gain profound insights into the diverse motivations, needs, and desires driving consumer behaviour. This enables more tailored and effective marketing strategies, as brands can craft messaging, products, and experiences that resonate with each specific cluster's psychological inclinations. Cluster analysis not only enhances brand engagement but also aids in the creation of emotionally resonant connections, ultimately fostering brand loyalty and growth by addressing the intricacies of human psychology that guide purchasing decisions.

Identifying Consumer Segments Based on Psychological Traits

This involves a sophisticated approach to market segmentation that goes beyond demographics. By delving into the intricate world of consumers' psychological characteristics, values, beliefs, and behavioural tendencies, brands gain a deeper understanding of what drives their target audience. This method recognizes that individuals within a demographic group can have vastly different motivations and preferences due to their unique psychological makeup. By grouping consumers with similar psychological traits into segments, brands can tailor their strategies to resonate with the underlying psychological factors that influence purchasing decisions, resulting in more precise targeting and more effective marketing campaigns.

- **Psychographic Segmentation: Beyond Demographics**

Psychographic segmentation involves categorizing consumers based on shared psychological traits, behaviours, and values, going beyond traditional demographic factors. **Lululemon** employs this by targeting individuals who prioritize wellness and an active lifestyle, crafting products and messaging that align with their psychographic preferences, thereby establishing a strong emotional connection and fostering brand loyalty through shared values and aspirations.

- **Personality Traits and their Role in Segmenting Consumers**

Personality traits play a key role in segmenting consumers by grouping individuals with similar psychological characteristics, guiding their preferences and behaviours. **Apple** utilizes this by targeting tech-savvy and innovative consumers who value sleek design and cutting-edge features, aligning their products and marketing with these personality traits, resulting in a dedicated customer base that resonates with the brand's identity and values.

- **Utilizing Psychometric Instruments for Consumer Profiling**

Utilizing psychometric instruments involves employing validated psychological assessments to profile consumers based on personality traits, values, and preferences. **IKEA** incorporates this by creating a 'Style Profile' quiz on their website, helping customers identify their design preferences and enabling the brand to personalize product recommendations, enhancing the shopping experience and driving customer satisfaction through tailored offerings.

- **Linking Personality Traits to Brand Preferences and Behaviours**

Linking personality traits to brand preferences and behaviours involves identifying correlations between individual traits and their choices. **Red Bull** exemplifies this by targeting adventurous and risk-taking individuals who resonate with traits like excitement-seeking, aligning their brand image and marketing strategies to attract consumers who share these personality characteristics, thereby establishing a strong connection between the brand and its target audience's core traits.

Psychographic Clusters and Brand Preferences

Psychographic clusters represent distinct groups of consumers with shared psychological traits, values, and lifestyles. These clusters offer a nuanced understanding of consumer behaviour beyond traditional demographics, revealing the intricate motivations and aspirations that drive brand preferences. By identifying psychographic clusters, brands gain insights into the specific psychological factors that resonate with each group. This knowledge allows them to tailor their marketing efforts, messaging, and product offerings to align with the unique characteristics of each cluster. As a result, brands can foster deeper emotional connections, enhance consumer engagement, and build brand loyalty by appealing to the psychological traits that shape individual preferences within these clusters.

- **Lifestyle Clusters and their Connection to Brand Choices**

Lifestyle clusters group consumers based on shared interests, activities, and values, providing insights into their brand preferences. **REI (Recreational Equipment, Inc.)** resonates with the "Outdoor Enthusiast" lifestyle cluster by offering outdoor gear and experiences that align with their values, creating a strong connection that influences brand loyalty through shared lifestyles and interests.

- **VALS Framework: Segmenting Audiences Based on Values**

The VALS framework segments audiences according to their values, lifestyle preferences, and psychographics, aiding in targeted marketing strategies. **Subaru** appeals to the "Achievers" segment by emphasizing reliability and durability, aligning with their values of practicality and adventure, which effectively builds brand loyalty through shared values and preferences.

- **Developing Psychographic Profiles for Brand Targeting**

Developing psychographic profiles involves creating detailed portraits of consumers based on psychological traits, behaviours, and preferences, enabling precise brand targeting. **Nike** creates psychographic profiles of fitness enthusiasts who seek motivation and self-improvement, tailoring their messaging and products to connect on a deeper level, fostering brand loyalty through shared motivations and interests.

- **Tailoring Brand Messaging to Psychographic Segments**

Tailoring brand messaging to psychographic segments entails customizing communication to resonate with specific psychological traits and preferences. **Starbucks** adapts its messaging to resonate with the "Urban Explorer" segment, highlighting coffee as an experience that complements their cosmopolitan lifestyle, forging a connection that enhances brand engagement by aligning with the segment's values and preferences.

Emotional Resonance and Segment Engagement Strategies

Emotional resonance and segment engagement strategies are integral components of modern marketing that focus on connecting deeply with consumers on an emotional level. By understanding the unique values, aspirations, and emotional triggers of different consumer segments, brands can craft messaging, experiences, and products that resonate profoundly. This resonance fosters a sense of belonging and understanding, creating stronger bonds between consumers and the brand. Through tailored engagement strategies, brands can evoke specific emotions that align with each segment's desires, ultimately driving higher levels of engagement, brand loyalty, and advocacy.

- **Emotional Appeal and its Effect on Different Psychographic Segments**

Emotional appeal involves crafting messages that evoke specific emotions, tailored to resonate with diverse psychographic segments. **Dove** employs emotional appeal by celebrating diverse beauty standards, effectively resonating with the "Empowered Self-Care Advocates" segment and forging a strong connection through shared values, resulting in increased engagement and brand loyalty.

- **Creating Emotional Connections through Targeted Messaging**

Creating emotional connections involves tailoring messages to resonate with consumers' values, resulting in deeper brand engagement. **Pampers** does this by highlighting moments of bonding between parents and babies, resonating with the "Nurturing Families" segment and forging a lasting emotional connection that enhances brand loyalty through shared experiences and values.

- **Crafting Brand Stories Aligned with Psychographic Traits**

Crafting brand stories aligned with psychographic traits involves developing narratives that resonate with specific consumer characteristics and values. **Patagonia** exemplifies this by sharing stories of environmental activism and responsible consumption, connecting with the "Conscious Outdoor Explorers" segment and reinforcing brand loyalty through shared values and beliefs.

- **Building Trust and Loyalty within Specific Psychographic Clusters**

Building trust and loyalty within specific psychographic clusters involves tailoring strategies to resonate with their values, fostering deeper connections. **Whole Foods Market** establishes trust and loyalty among health-conscious consumers by offering organic products and promoting sustainable practices that align with the "Health and Sustainability Advocates" segment, strengthening brand loyalty through shared values and ethical considerations.

Cross-Cultural Differences in Psychographic Segments

Cross-cultural differences in psychographic segments refer to the variations in values, attitudes, and lifestyle preferences that emerge when analysing consumer groups from diverse cultural backgrounds. Cultural nuances, societal norms, and historical contexts shape psychographic profiles differently, influencing consumer motivations and behaviours across various regions and ethnicities. These differences emphasize the need for brands to adopt a culturally sensitive approach, crafting messaging and engagement strategies that respect and resonate with the unique psychographic traits of each cultural segment. Understanding and adapting to these variations not only deepens brand connections but also helps avoid misunderstandings or cultural insensitivities, fostering successful global marketing campaigns.

- **Cultural Influences on Psychological Needs and Traits**

Cultural influences shape psychological needs and traits, leading to variations in consumer behaviours and preferences across different societies. **McDonald's** adapts its menu offerings in different countries, recognizing cultural differences in dietary preferences and values, aligning its brand with local psychographic traits to effectively connect with diverse audiences and build stronger brand relationships.

146

- **Adapting Psychographic Segmentation for Global Audiences**

Adapting psychographic segmentation for global audiences involves recognizing cultural variations and tailoring strategies to resonate with diverse psychological traits and values. **Coca-Cola** adjusts its marketing campaigns to reflect regional cultural values while maintaining its brand identity, effectively connecting with consumers worldwide by considering their unique psychographic profiles and fostering a sense of familiarity and relevance.

- **Balancing Cultural Nuances with Universal Human Motivations**

Balancing cultural nuances with universal human motivations entails crafting strategies that resonate globally by addressing common psychological needs while respecting cultural differences. **Nike** strikes this balance by promoting self-expression and determination, universal values, while adapting campaigns to local cultures, fostering a strong emotional connection that spans cultures by appealing to shared and culturally sensitive motivations.

Neuromarketing Insights in Segment Analysis

Neuromarketing insights play a pivotal role in segment analysis by uncovering subconscious reactions and emotional triggers that drive consumer behaviour. Through techniques such as brain imaging and physiological measurements, businesses gain a deeper understanding of how different segments respond to marketing stimuli. These insights provide a more comprehensive picture of consumers' motivations, preferences, and decision-making processes, allowing for the creation of highly targeted strategies that resonate on a profound level. By aligning messaging, products, and experiences with the neurological and emotional inclinations of specific segments, brands can enhance engagement, build stronger connections, and ultimately drive more effective marketing campaigns.

- **Neuro Metrics for Psychographic Segment Profiling**

Neuro metrics involve using neurological measurements to profile psychographic segments, revealing subconscious reactions and preferences. **PepsiCo** employed neuro metrics to analyse consumers' brain responses to different product packaging designs, gaining insights into the preferences of specific segments and tailoring their packaging to resonate with the underlying psychological traits, enhancing engagement and brand affinity through precise targeting.

- **Neural Responses to Different Brand Messages by Segments**

Studying neural responses to various brand messages across segments involves using brain imaging to understand subconscious reactions. **Doritos** conducted a study using neuroimaging to analyse responses to different ad messages among different segments, leading to the creation of messages that resonated strongly with each segment's underlying psychological traits, resulting in more impactful and engaging marketing efforts.

- **Neural Mechanisms Underlying Segment Engagement**

Neural mechanisms underlying segment engagement involve uncovering how specific brain processes influence consumers' reactions and preferences within segments. **Netflix** utilizes this by analysing viewers' brain activity patterns to optimize content recommendations, aligning with each viewer's neural responses and enhancing engagement through personalized viewing suggestions that resonate with their individual preferences.

- **Enhancing Segment-Specific Communication using Neuro Insights**

Enhancing segment-specific communication through neuro insights involves tailoring messaging based on subconscious responses. **BMW** employed neuro insights to craft emotionally resonant advertisements for different segments, connecting with their underlying psychological traits and preferences, resulting in more compelling messaging that resonated deeply with each segment and enhanced brand engagement.

Targeted Persuasion for Psychographic Clusters

Targeted persuasion for psychographic clusters refers to the strategic approach of tailoring persuasive messaging and communication to resonate specifically with distinct groups of consumers who share similar psychological traits, values, and preferences. By understanding the unique motivations and triggers of each psychographic cluster, brands can craft messages that deeply connect with their core desires and emotions. This personalized approach increases the likelihood of capturing attention, evoking emotional responses, and ultimately influencing purchasing decisions. By aligning persuasive strategies with the psychological nuances of each segment, brands can effectively engage consumers and foster stronger brand loyalty by addressing their individual needs and aspirations.

- **Persuasion Tactics Aligned with Psychographic Traits**

Persuasion tactics aligned with psychographic traits involve tailoring communication strategies to resonate with specific consumer motivations. **H&M** employs this by using social media influencers who embody the style preferences and values of the "Fashion Enthusiast" segment, effectively engaging this group through relatable and aspirational content that aligns with their psychographic traits, thus influencing their purchasing decisions and brand loyalty.

- **Matching Message Framing to Segment Motivations**

Matching message framing to segment motivations involves presenting content in a way that aligns with each group's psychological drivers. **Nike** adeptly does this by using empowerment-focused messaging for the "Achievement-Driven Athletes" segment and sustainability-oriented messaging for the "Environmentally Conscious" segment, creating a powerful connection through messages that resonate with their unique motivations, and thereby strengthening their brand engagement and loyalty.

- **Leveraging Social Proof within Specific Consumer Clusters**

Leveraging social proof within specific consumer clusters involves using endorsements and references from individuals within those segments to influence their choices. **Airbnb** effectively utilizes this by showcasing reviews and recommendations from hosts and guests who align with the preferences of the "Adventure Seekers" segment, creating a sense of trust and validation that resonates with their psychographic traits, ultimately enhancing brand credibility and engagement within this group.

- ## Ethical Considerations in Targeting Vulnerable Segments

Ethical considerations in targeting vulnerable segments involve ensuring that marketing strategies do not exploit or harm consumers who may be more susceptible. **McDonald's** faced criticism for targeting children with colourful branding and toys, highlighting the importance of responsibly aligning marketing tactics with the well-being of vulnerable segments, and emphasizing the need for ethical safeguards when engaging such audiences.

Branding to Multiple Psychographic Segments

Branding to multiple psychographic segments involves creating a cohesive yet tailored brand identity that resonates with diverse groups of consumers based on their unique psychological traits, values, and preferences. By understanding the distinct motivations and aspirations of each segment, brands can develop messaging, products, and experiences that evoke emotional connections and foster a sense of belonging. This approach acknowledges the multifaceted nature of consumers and strives to create a brand that not only reflects shared values within each segment but also unifies them under a broader brand narrative, resulting in increased engagement, loyalty, and a more inclusive brand image.

- ## Creating Brand Narratives with Multifaceted Appeal

Creating brand narratives with multifaceted appeal involves crafting stories that resonate with various psychographic segments' unique traits and values. **Nike** excels at this by promoting both the spirit of individual achievement for the "Ambitious Athletes" segment and the message of inclusivity for the "Community-Driven Advocates" segment, creating a holistic brand narrative that speaks to diverse consumer motivations and fostering a broader and more resonant brand identity.

- **Managing Perceptions Across Different Segment Preferences**

Managing perceptions across different segment preferences requires maintaining a consistent brand image while adapting messaging to align with diverse psychological traits. **Starbucks** achieves this by offering both cozy atmospheres for the "Comfort-Seeking" segment and trendy spaces for the "Urban Explorers," ensuring a unified brand perception while catering to distinct preferences, which fosters a positive perception among various psychographic clusters.

- **Brand Architecture for Multi-Brand Strategies**

Brand architecture for multi-brand strategies involves structuring and organizing multiple brands within a portfolio to maximize synergies and cater to different segments. **Procter & Gamble (P&G)** employs this by having distinct brands like **Pampers** and **Tide** under its umbrella, each tailored to specific consumer segments, enabling efficient targeting and resource allocation while ensuring a cohesive brand strategy across various psychographic clusters.

CROSS-CULTURAL BRAND PSYCHOLOGY: NAVIGATING DIVERSE MARKETS

Cross-cultural brand psychology navigates the intricate landscape of diverse markets by delving into the intersections of culture, consumer behaviour, and brand strategies. As global markets become increasingly interconnected, understanding how cultural nuances shape consumer perceptions, preferences, and interactions with brands is paramount. This interdisciplinary approach draws insights from psychology, sociology, and marketing to unravel how cultural dimensions influence individuals' psychological processes, impacting their perceptions of brands and consumption patterns. Acknowledging that culture shapes not only consumer behaviour but also brand meaning and identity, cross-cultural brand psychology guides businesses in adapting their strategies to resonate authentically with local values and norms. By fostering sensitivity to cultural diversity, brands can forge stronger connections, establish trust, and effectively navigate the multifaceted landscape of global markets, ultimately securing a competitive edge in today's complex and interconnected business environment.

Cultural Dimensions and Brand Perception

Cultural dimensions and brand perception explore the profound impact of cultural values, norms, and practices on how consumers perceive and interact with brands. These dimensions, such as individualism-collectivism, power distance, and uncertainty avoidance, shape the lenses through which individuals interpret brand messages, attributes, and symbolism. By recognizing and adapting to these cultural nuances, brands can strategically tailor their positioning, messaging, and imagery to align with the values and expectations of specific cultures. This approach not only enhances brand relevance but also fosters deeper emotional connections, enabling brands to resonate more authentically and effectively with diverse audiences across different cultural landscapes.

- **Hofstede's Cultural Dimensions and Their Branding Implications**

Hofstede's cultural dimensions offer insights into how cultural values influence consumer behaviours, impacting brand perception and strategies. **McDonald's** adapts its menu offerings and advertising tone in India, where collectivism and high power distance are prominent, demonstrating how cultural dimensions guide branding choices to resonate with cultural values and enhance brand acceptance and loyalty within specific cultural contexts.

- **Individualism vs. Collectivism in Shaping Brand Relationships**

Individualism vs. collectivism influences brand relationships, as individualistic cultures emphasize personal aspirations while collectivist cultures prioritize group harmony. **Coca-Cola** promotes a sense of togetherness and shared moments in its advertising campaigns, catering to collectivist tendencies and forging stronger brand connections by resonating with cultural values that prioritize community and unity.

- **Power Distance and Its Influence on Brand Communication**

Power distance impacts brand communication, as cultures with high power distance respect authority, while low power distance cultures value equality. **Toyota** employs this by adapting its advertising tone in different regions; in high power distance cultures, they may emphasize authority figures' endorsements, whereas,f in low power distance cultures, they emphasize collaborative decision-making, aligning their communication with cultural norms to establish effective brand connections.

- **Masculinity vs. Femininity in Crafting Brand Identity**

Masculinity vs. femininity influences brand identity, as cultures prioritize traits like assertiveness (masculine) or nurturing (feminine). **Dove** appeals to femininity by celebrating natural beauty, aligning with nurturing values and crafting a brand identity that resonates with cultural norms, reinforcing emotional connections and brand loyalty among feminine-focused segments.

Cultural Symbols and Semiotics in Branding

Cultural symbols and semiotics are pivotal elements in branding, encompassing visual, verbal, and symbolic cues that communicate profound meanings within specific cultural contexts. These symbols hold deep cultural associations and emotional significance, allowing brands to tap into shared values, beliefs, and narratives. By incorporating culturally resonant symbols, colours, and imagery, brands can establish immediate connections with consumers, evoke emotional responses, and convey their essence in a nuanced manner. This approach not only bridges language barriers but also aligns with cultural codes, strengthening brand relevance and engagement while fostering deeper connections that transcend linguistic and cultural boundaries.

- **Cultural Symbols and Their Significance in Branding**

Cultural symbols play a crucial role in branding by carrying deep cultural meanings that resonate with specific audiences. **Nike** utilizes the "swoosh" symbol, representing movement and progress, across cultures, effectively using a universally recognizable cultural symbol to communicate the brand's core values and aspirations, fostering a global connection that transcends language and resonates with diverse audiences.

- **Adapting Symbolic Brand Associations for Different Cultures**

Adapting symbolic brand associations involves tailoring imagery and symbols to align with cultural interpretations. **KFC** modifies its branding by using chopsticks in its logo in China, aligning with local eating habits and creating a cultural resonance that enhances brand familiarity and connection, highlighting how adapting symbols to cultural nuances ensures that branding resonates authentically and establishes relatable associations within specific cultural markets.

- **Cross-Cultural Semiotics: Balancing Universality with Cultural Nuances**

Cross-cultural semiotics involves striking a balance between symbols that hold universal meanings and those that carry cultural nuances. **Apple** employs a simple, minimalist design that conveys universality while subtly adapting its marketing imagery to local customs, achieving a harmonious blend that resonates across diverse cultures, highlighting the importance of semiotic strategies that can communicate core brand messages while respecting cultural differences.

- **Localizing Brand Communication Through Symbolic Adaptation**

Localizing brand communication involves adapting symbols to align with local cultural interpretations, enhancing relatability. **Coca-Cola** tailors its logo with characters from various languages, like Arabic and Chinese, maintaining brand recognition while demonstrating cultural sensitivity, ultimately reinforcing positive brand perception by adapting symbols to local preferences and interpretations.

Transcreation and Multilingual Branding

Transcreation and multilingual branding encompass the art of adapting brand messages across languages and cultures while maintaining the intended emotional impact and essence. Unlike simple translation, transcreation involves recreating content to resonate with the cultural nuances, linguistic subtleties, and emotional triggers of each target audience. By carefully crafting messages that evoke the same feelings and responses in different languages, brands can maintain their authenticity, connect on a deeper level, and foster consistent emotional associations across diverse markets, ultimately ensuring a unified brand experience that transcends linguistic barriers.

- **Transcreation: Beyond Translation for Cross-Cultural Appeal**

Transcreation goes beyond translation by adapting content to resonate culturally, ensuring cross-cultural appeal.

McDonald's translated its slogan "I'm lovin' it" to "Me encanta" in Spanish-speaking markets, maintaining the essence of the message while considering cultural idiomatic expressions, exemplifying how transcreation preserves brand essence while connecting authentically with diverse audiences by addressing cultural nuances.

- **The Role of Language in Building Cultural Brand Connections**

Language plays a pivotal role in establishing cultural brand connections by enabling direct and relatable communication. **IKEA** offers product names in local languages in different countries, forming linguistic bonds that resonate with consumers on a personal level, effectively using language as a bridge to connect with diverse cultural segments and strengthen brand engagement through linguistic familiarity and relatability.

- **Navigating Wordplay, Puns, and Cultural Idioms in Branding**

Navigating wordplay, puns, and cultural idioms in branding involves using language humor that resonates culturally. **Kit Kat** used the tagline "Have a Break, Have a Kit Kat" in the UK, incorporating a pun on "break" to convey both a snack and a pause, effectively using language play to create a memorable and culturally relevant message that resonates with local consumers by tapping into linguistic familiarity and cultural context.

Colour Psychology Across Cultures

Colour psychology across cultures explores the profound impact of colour on human emotions, perceptions, and behaviours within diverse cultural contexts. Colours carry deep cultural associations and symbolism that can differ significantly from one society to another, shaping how individuals interpret brands, products, and communication. As a result, understanding the cross-cultural nuances of colour preferences and meanings is crucial for creating effective and resonant branding strategies. By recognizing the cultural significance of colours, businesses can craft visual identities that evoke the intended emotional responses and establish connections with consumers across global markets, ultimately enhancing brand engagement and fostering a more culturally sensitive and relevant brand presence.

- **The Influence of Colours on Cultural Perceptions and Meanings**

The influence of colours on cultural perceptions and meanings lies in how different colours evoke specific emotions and carry diverse symbolism within various cultural contexts, shaping consumer interpretations and attitudes towards brands and products.

- **Cultural Variability in Colour Associations and Symbolism**

Cultural variability in colour associations and symbolism emphasizes how colours hold diverse meanings and emotions across cultures, impacting consumer responses and brand perceptions.

- **Adapting Colour Palettes for Cross-Cultural Branding**

Adapting colour palettes for cross-cultural branding involves tailoring visual elements to align with cultural preferences and interpretations, ensuring resonance and relevance across diverse markets.

- **Avoiding Colour Misinterpretations in Global Markets**

Avoiding colour misinterpretations in global markets requires thorough research to understand cultural connotations and ensuring that chosen colours align positively with local perceptions, preventing potential misunderstandings or negative associations.

Localizing Brand Communication Strategies

Localizing brand communication strategies involves tailoring marketing approaches to resonate authentically with the cultural, linguistic, and social nuances of specific markets. By adapting messaging, imagery, and promotional tactics to align with local preferences and values, businesses can break down barriers, build trust, and create a more meaningful connection with consumers in different regions. This approach recognizes that effective communication goes beyond translation, encompassing the integration of cultural context and sensitivities to ensure that messages are not only understood but also genuinely embraced by the target audience. Ultimately, successful localization enhances brand relevance, engagement, and loyalty in diverse markets by catering to the distinctive traits and expectations of each region.

- **The Importance of Contextualization in Brand Messaging**

The importance of contextualization in brand messaging lies in its ability to adapt messages to specific cultural, social, and linguistic contexts, ensuring that communications resonate authentically and effectively with diverse audiences. This approach enhances comprehension, emotional connection, and brand relevance in different markets.**McDonald's** tailors its menu offerings and messaging to cater to local preferences, highlighting the significance of contextualization in cross-cultural branding strategies.

- **Adapting Brand Communication to Local Sensitivities**

Adapting brand communication to local sensitivities involves crafting messages that respect cultural norms and values, ensuring a positive reception. **PepsiCo** faced backlash in Thailand due to a campaign that was perceived as culturally insensitive, underscoring the importance of aligning communication with local sensibilities to avoid unintended offense and maintain a favourable brand image within specific cultural contexts.

- **Customizing Marketing Channels for Cultural Relevance**

Customizing marketing channels for cultural relevance entails selecting platforms that resonate with local preferences and behaviours. **Unilever** utilizes social media influencers from specific regions to connect with audiences on platforms popular in those areas, demonstrating how adapting marketing channels enhances cultural resonance and consumer engagement by aligning with local communication habits and preferences.

- **Balancing Global Brand Consistency with Local Adaptations**

Balancing global brand consistency with local adaptations involves maintaining core brand identity while tailoring strategies to suit diverse markets. **Starbucks** maintains its signature ambiance while offering region-specific menu items, exemplifying how a harmonious blend ensures brand recognition while catering to local tastes, achieving a balance that resonates globally while addressing local preferences for a stronger and more adaptable brand presence.

Cultural Norms and Brand Trust

Cultural norms and brand trust are intertwined elements that influence consumer perceptions and interactions. Cultural norms encompass shared societal beliefs, values, and behaviours that shape consumer expectations and decision-making processes. Brands that align with these norms foster a sense of familiarity, credibility, and relatability, enhancing trust among consumers. By acknowledging and respecting cultural norms, brands can establish a genuine connection with their target audience, leading to higher levels of trust and loyalty. This approach acknowledges the importance of understanding and adapting to local cultural nuances, ensuring that brand messaging, actions, and values resonate authentically within specific cultural contexts and reinforce consumer trust.

- **Trust-Building Strategies Tailored to Cultural Norms**

Trust-building strategies tailored to cultural norms involve crafting approaches that resonate with local values, enhancing brand credibility. **Toyota** focuses on reliability and longevity, aligning with the cultural emphasis on durability in Japanese society, exemplifying how adapting trust-building strategies to cultural norms reinforces authenticity and strengthens consumer trust by reflecting values that resonate within the culture.

- **Overcoming Cultural Skepticism and Mistrust**

Overcoming cultural skepticism and mistrust requires brands to address historical, social, or economic factors that breed distrust, and to build transparent and consistent relationships. **Nestlé** faced mistrust in India due to concerns about water usage, prompting the brand to focus on sustainable practices and transparent communication to rebuild trust and demonstrate a commitment to addressing cultural sensitivities, showing how overcoming skepticism requires brands to understand cultural concerns and implement strategies that align with local values and expectations.

- **Building Long-Term Trust Through Respectful Cultural Engagement**

Building long-term trust through respectful cultural engagement involves consistently demonstrating genuine interest and understanding of cultural values. **Google** offers localized search experiences and language support in various countries, reflecting a commitment to respecting local cultural contexts, highlighting how brands that engage respectfully and authentically over time can establish trust by demonstrating their willingness to adapt and connect with diverse cultural communities on their own terms.

- **Case Studies in Brands Establishing Cross-Cultural Trust**

Case studies in brands establishing cross-cultural trust exemplify how tailored strategies create meaningful connections. **Airbnb** features hosts from different cultures in its campaigns, promoting inclusivity and showcasing its commitment to building trust across cultural boundaries, illustrating how fostering trust requires cultural sensitivity and personal connections that resonate with diverse audiences, ultimately enhancing brand credibility and engagement.

Globalization and Glocalization in Branding

Globalization and glocalization in branding represent the intricate balance between extending a brand's reach across international borders while maintaining a local, personalized appeal. Globalization involves expanding a brand's presence worldwide through consistent strategies, visuals, and messaging. Glocalization, on the other hand, recognizes the importance of adapting these elements to align with local preferences, cultural nuances, and market peculiarities. This approach acknowledges that while global consistency builds brand recognition, local relevance fosters emotional connections. Successful brands seamlessly blend global and local elements, respecting diverse cultures while retaining a unified brand identity, leading to effective market penetration, engagement, and lasting brand loyalty in an increasingly interconnected world.

- **The Balance Between Global Consistency and Local Relevance**

The balance between global consistency and local relevance involves harmonizing a standardized brand identity with culturally tailored strategies. **McDonald's** maintains its core menu worldwide while adapting offerings to suit local tastes, demonstrating how aligning with this balance enhances recognition while catering to cultural preferences, resulting in a cohesive yet adaptable brand presence that resonates across diverse markets.

- **Glocalization Strategies for Resonance in Diverse Markets**

Glocalization strategies aim to create resonance in diverse markets by combining global elements with localized adaptations. **Coca-Cola** tailors its flavors and packaging to match local preferences and customs while maintaining its global brand identity, illustrating how glocalization enables brands to engage with cultural diversity, enhance relevance, and establish a strong and adaptable market presence that resonates both locally and globally.

- **Local Adaptation of Brand Identity and Values**

Local adaptation of brand identity and values involves tailoring core brand attributes to align with cultural sensibilities and preferences. **IKEA** adjusts its product offerings and store layouts to suit local lifestyles and spatial norms, reflecting how localized adaptations respect cultural nuances while maintaining brand integrity, leading to enhanced resonance and relevance within specific markets.

INNOVATION AND FUTURE TRENDS IN NEURO MARKETING AND COGNITIVE PSYCHOLOGY IN BRANDING

Innovation and future trends in neuro marketing and cognitive psychology are poised to revolutionize branding strategies by offering deeper insights into consumer behaviour and preferences. Advancements in neuroimaging techniques, such as fMRI and EEG, are unlocking the ability to uncover subconscious reactions and emotional responses, allowing brands to create more resonant and impactful messaging. Additionally, the integration of artificial intelligence and machine learning can analyse vast datasets of cognitive and emotional responses, predicting consumer behaviours and enabling more personalized and effective marketing campaigns. As the field progresses, a more holistic understanding of how the human brain processes information, makes decisions, and forms brand associations will drive the development of strategies that appeal to consumers on a fundamental level, creating powerful and enduring brand-consumer connections.

Evolving Approaches in Neuro Marketing for Branding

Evolving approaches in neuro marketing are reshaping branding strategies, as they delve into the subconscious aspects of consumer decision-making. The integration of neuroscience and psychology allows brands to move beyond traditional market research, gaining insights into emotional triggers, cognitive processes, and even non-conscious associations that influence brand perception. These insights enable the creation of tailored and emotionally resonant messaging, ensuring a deeper connection with consumers. As technology advances, wearable devices and biometric measurements can provide real-time data on physiological responses, offering a more comprehensive understanding of consumer reactions. This evolving landscape is steering brands toward a more nuanced and scientifically grounded approach, ensuring that branding efforts are not only captivating but also rooted in a deeper understanding of human psychology.

- **Advancements in Brain Imaging Techniques for Consumer Insights**

Advancements in brain imaging techniques, like fMRI and EEG, offer brands direct access to subconscious consumer reactions, enabling precise tailoring of messaging and strategies for stronger emotional connections and resonant branding. These techniques illuminate the neural underpinnings of consumer behaviour, bridging the gap between neuroscience and marketing for more effective and targeted engagement.

- **Real-Time Neuro Feedback: Adapting Brand Messages on the Fly**

Real-time neuro feedback enables brands to dynamically adjust messages based on consumers' real-time neurological responses, ensuring immediate alignment with their emotional engagement and cognitive reactions. **Amazon** utilizes real-time user data to tailor product recommendations, demonstrating how this approach can adapt brand experiences to individual preferences in real-time, fostering deeper connections and enhancing overall consumer satisfaction.

- **Combining Neuro Metrics with Traditional Market Research**

Combining neuro metrics with traditional market research integrates objective neurological data with qualitative insights, providing a holistic understanding of consumer behaviour. **PepsiCo** combined EEG measurements with focus groups to assess the impact of packaging design on consumer preferences, illustrating how this approach offers comprehensive insights into both subconscious and conscious responses, guiding branding decisions and enhancing product appeal by incorporating both scientific and qualitative perspectives.

- **Ethical Considerations in Gathering Neuro Data for Branding**

Ethical considerations in gathering neuro data for branding entail ensuring informed consent, privacy, and responsible data usage. **Facebook** faced scrutiny over privacy concerns related to user data, underlining the importance of transparent practices and stringent ethical guidelines in the collection and utilization of neuro data for branding, emphasizing the need for brands to prioritize consumer trust and uphold ethical standards while harnessing neuroscience insights for marketing strategies.

Neuromarketing and Emotional Branding

Neuromarketing intersects with emotional branding by uncovering the subconscious emotional triggers that influence consumer choices, enabling brands to craft more emotionally resonant messaging and experiences for deeper brand connections.

- **Mapping Neural Responses to Emotional Branding Stimuli**

Mapping neural responses to emotional branding stimuli involves using neuroimaging techniques to observe how the brain reacts to emotionally charged content, unveiling insights into the subconscious emotional processes that drive consumer engagement and shaping more effective emotional branding strategies.

- **Identifying Universal Emotional Triggers Across Cultures**

Identifying universal emotional triggers across cultures involves pinpointing emotional stimuli that evoke consistent responses regardless of cultural differences, allowing brands to create emotionally resonant content that transcends cultural boundaries and connects with diverse audiences on a fundamental emotional level.

- **Emotionally Engaging Storytelling: A Neuro-Psychological Approach**

Emotionally engaging storytelling employs neuro-psychological insights to create narratives that resonate deeply with audiences, stimulating emotional centers of the brain and forming lasting connections. By aligning storytelling with cognitive and emotional processes, brands can forge stronger bonds and leave a lasting impact on consumers' perceptions and preferences. This approach acknowledges the power of storytelling in leveraging human psychology for effective brand communication.

- **Personalized Emotional Branding through Neuro Insights**

Personalized emotional branding leverages neuro insights to tailor brand experiences that align with individual emotional triggers, resulting in more impactful and relevant connections. By understanding consumers' subconscious responses, brands can deliver tailored messaging and interactions that resonate deeply, fostering brand loyalty and emotional resonance. This approach underscores the potential of neuroscience to guide the customization of emotional branding strategies for heightened consumer engagement.

Neuro Metrics for Social Media Branding

Neuro metrics have emerged as a transformative tool in the realm of social media branding, offering a window into consumers' subconscious reactions and emotional engagement with brand content. By applying neuroimaging techniques such as EEG and fMRI to social media interactions, brands can decode users' neurological responses to posts, videos, and advertisements. This enables a more nuanced understanding of how different elements – from visuals and language to storytelling – impact consumer emotions and perceptions. With this real-time insight, brands can refine their social media strategies, ensuring that content resonates on a deeper emotional level and drives stronger engagement. Additionally, the integration of neuro metrics with social media analytics allows for precise measurement of consumers' attention, emotional intensity, and memory retention, providing brands with the data necessary to optimize their social media campaigns for maximum impact. As the digital landscape evolves, harnessing the power of neuro metrics in social media branding promises to create more authentic and resonant connections between brands and consumers.

- **Analysing Neural Responses to Social Media Content**

Analysing neural responses to social media content involves using neuroimaging techniques to study how the brain reacts to posts, videos, and ads, providing insights into subconscious emotional engagement and cognitive processing. For instance, brands like **Doritos** can measure users' brain responses to different ad campaigns on platforms like Instagram, helping tailor content to evoke stronger emotional connections and optimize the impact of their social media branding efforts.

- **Measuring Emotional Engagement through Neuro Metrics**

Measuring emotional engagement through neuro metrics entails utilizing tools such as EEG and fMRI to quantify consumers' emotional responses to brand content. For instance, **Nike** could use these metrics to evaluate the emotional impact of their social media campaigns, enabling them to refine their messaging and visuals for heightened resonance and improved emotional connection with their audience.

- **Predicting Viral Content Using Neuro Insights**

Predicting viral content using neuro insights involves analysing brain responses to determine the elements that resonate deeply and have the potential for widespread sharing. For example, **Red Bull** could use neuro metrics to assess the neural reactions to different video campaigns, helping them identify the content characteristics that lead to higher emotional engagement and shareability, ultimately guiding their efforts to create more viral-worthy social media content.

- **The Neuro Psychology of Building Online Brand Communities**

The neuro psychology of building online brand communities delves into the cognitive and emotional drivers behind individuals' participation in digital brand communities. For instance, **Apple's** online community thrives by tapping into users' shared passion for the brand's products, triggering a sense of identity and emotional attachment, showcasing how understanding the neuro psychology of online interactions can foster a strong sense of community and brand loyalty.

AI and Predictive Neuromarketing in Branding

AI and predictive neuromarketing are converging to reshape the branding landscape by offering advanced insights into consumer behaviour. Leveraging AI algorithms and machine learning, brands can analyse vast amounts of neuro data to predict consumer responses to various stimuli, enabling them to create more tailored and resonant branding strategies. By predicting emotional triggers and cognitive preferences, brands can optimize their messaging, design, and product offerings to effectively engage customers. This symbiotic relationship between AI and neuromarketing empowers brands to proactively anticipate consumer reactions, enhancing the precision and impact of their branding efforts and ultimately fostering stronger emotional connections with their audience.

• AI-Powered Neuromarketing Algorithms for Consumer Insights

AI-powered neuromarketing algorithms leverage machine learning to analyse neuro data, providing in-depth consumer insights. For instance, companies like **Netflix** utilize these algorithms to predict viewer preferences based on neural reactions, enhancing their content recommendation systems and personalizing the user experience. This integration of AI and neuromarketing exemplifies how predictive algorithms can decode subconscious responses, guiding brands to tailor their strategies for more effective and resonant consumer engagement.

• Predicting Consumer Behaviour through Neuro Data Analysis

Predicting consumer behaviour through neuro data analysis involves using advanced techniques to decode subconscious responses and anticipate consumer preferences. **Amazon** employs predictive neuro data analysis to forecast product demand based on brain reactions to different offerings, optimizing their inventory and enhancing customer satisfaction. This approach showcases how analysing neural responses can yield valuable insights, enabling brands to proactively shape their strategies and offerings in alignment with consumer preferences.

• Automated Personalization through AI-Driven Neuro Insights

Automated personalization through AI-driven neuro insights represents the future of branding, where algorithms analyse neural responses to deliver highly tailored experiences. Imagine a scenario where **Nike** uses AI to analyse consumers' neurological reactions to different shoe designs, enabling the brand to automatically customize product recommendations and design elements for each individual, creating a seamless blend of neuroscience and AI for unparalleled personalization that resonates deeply with consumers.

- **Challenges in Ensuring AI-Generated Insights' Accuracy and Validity**

Challenges in ensuring AI-generated insights' accuracy and validity arise from potential biases and misinterpretations within the algorithms. For instance, **Google's** AI photo tagging feature misidentified people of colour due to biased training data. This highlights the importance of rigorous data curation and constant validation to prevent skewed or inaccurate insights, underscoring the need for brands to critically assess and fine-tune AI-driven solutions to ensure ethical and precise outcomes in their branding strategies.

Generative AI and Innovative Brand Storytelling

Generative AI is revolutionizing innovative brand storytelling by enabling brands to create dynamic and personalized narratives. With generative AI, brands can craft unique and engaging stories that adapt in real-time to individual preferences and contexts. For example, a luxury car brand like **Mercedes-Benz** could use generative AI to create interactive virtual showrooms where customers explore different car features based on their interests, providing an immersive and personalized brand experience that goes beyond traditional linear storytelling. This fusion of AI and storytelling offers brands a powerful tool to captivate audiences and create memorable brand interactions.

- **Exploring Generative AI for Crafting Unique Brand Narratives**

Exploring generative AI for crafting unique brand narratives involves utilizing AI algorithms to generate creative and personalized storytelling experiences. Brands can harness generative AI to dynamically create narratives that resonate with individual consumers' preferences and emotions. For instance, a fashion brand like **Gucci** could use generative AI to craft customized fashion journey stories based on users' style preferences, enhancing engagement and forming deeper connections through tailored brand storytelling. This innovative approach offers brands the ability to captivate audiences with narratives that feel tailored specifically to them, elevating the brand-consumer relationship.

- **Customizing Stories for Diverse Consumer Neuro Profiles**

Customizing stories for diverse consumer neuro profiles entails tailoring narratives based on individual neural responses and preferences. By analysing neuro data, brands can create storytelling elements that resonate with specific cognitive and emotional patterns. For instance, a tech company like **Apple** could adjust their product launch narratives using neuro insights to match different consumer neuro profiles, resulting in more emotionally engaging and compelling brand stories that effectively resonate across a diverse audience. This approach showcases the potential of customization driven by neuroscience to enhance brand storytelling strategies and optimize consumer engagement.

- **Enhancing Emotional Resonance through AI-Generated Story Elements**

Enhancing emotional resonance through AI-generated story elements involves leveraging AI to craft narrative components that evoke strong emotional connections. By analysing emotional triggers and preferences from neuro data, brands can create characters, settings, and plot twists that resonate deeply with audiences. For example, a food brand like **Ben & Jerry's** could use AI to generate storylines that align with consumers' emotional associations with their ice cream flavors, heightening the emotional impact of their brand narratives and fostering a more profound connection between the audience and the brand. This fusion of AI and emotional storytelling amplifies the effectiveness of brand narratives, elevating the overall brand experience.

- **Maintaining Brand Authenticity Amid AI-Generated Creativity**

Maintaining brand authenticity amid AI-generated creativity involves carefully curating AI-generated content to align with the brand's core values and identity. While AI can enhance creativity, brands must ensure that the generated content reflects their unique voice and resonates with their audience authentically. For instance, a heritage brand like **Coca-Cola** could use AI to create innovative advertisements while preserving the nostalgic essence that defines their identity, demonstrating the challenge and importance of balancing AI-generated creativity with the brand's established authenticity. This approach underscores the need for brands to strike a harmonious balance between leveraging AI's capabilities and staying true to their brand essence.

Neuro-AI Integration for Hyper-Personalization

Neuro-AI integration for hyper-personalization involves combining neuroscience insights with AI-driven algorithms to create deeply personalized experiences. By analysing neuro data, brands can better understand individual preferences and emotional responses, allowing AI systems to tailor content and interactions in real time. For example, an online retailer like **Amazon** could use neuro-AI integration to customize product recommendations based on consumers' subconscious reactions, enhancing the level of personalization and driving higher engagement by delivering content that resonates on a more profound cognitive and emotional level. This fusion of neuroscience and AI enables brands to forge stronger connections with consumers through experiences that feel intimately attuned to their individual preferences and emotions.

- **Integrating AI-Generated Insights with Neuromarketing Data**

Integrating AI-generated insights with neuromarketing data involves combining the analytical power of AI with the deep emotional understanding provided by neuro data. By merging these insights, brands can gain a comprehensive understanding of consumer behaviour, preferences, and emotional responses. For instance, a cosmetic brand like **L'Oréal** could integrate AI-generated insights about beauty trends with neuromarketing data on emotional reactions to specific cosmetic products, enabling them to create targeted marketing campaigns that resonate both intellectually and emotionally with their audience. This integration showcases how the synergy between AI and neuromarketing can elevate brands' understanding of their customers and refine their strategies for maximum impact.

- **Achieving Hyper-Personalized Brand Communication**

Achieving hyper-personalized brand communication involves leveraging data-driven insights from AI and neuromarketing to create tailored messages that deeply resonate with individual consumers. By analysing both cognitive preferences and emotional triggers, brands can craft messages that speak to consumers' unique needs and desires. For instance, an e-commerce platform like **eBay** could use AI and neuromarketing data to deliver personalized product recommendations that align with consumers' cognitive preferences and emotional responses, resulting in a more impactful and relevant communication strategy that fosters stronger brand-consumer relationships. This approach underscores the potential of hyper-personalization to enhance the overall brand experience by creating connections that are not only highly personalized but also emotionally resonant.

- **Predicting Individual Receptivity to Different Brand Messages**

Predicting individual receptivity to different brand messages involves using AI and neuromarketing to analyse neuro data and past behavioural patterns, enabling brands to anticipate how specific messages will emotionally and cognitively resonate with each consumer. By combining insights from both fields, brands can tailor their communication strategies to deliver messages that align with individual preferences and emotional triggers. For instance, a technology company like **Apple** could predict which features of a new product would engage different customers based on their neural responses, resulting in more effective and personalized marketing campaigns that enhance the likelihood of positive consumer responses. This integration exemplifies the potential of combining AI and neuromarketing to optimize message delivery and consumer engagement.

- **Ethical and privacy concerns in hyper-personalization**

Ethical and privacy concerns in hyper-personalization arise due to the extensive collection of individual data and potential manipulation of consumer behaviours. Combining AI and neuromarketing data to achieve hyper-personalization requires careful consideration of consent, transparency, and data security. For instance, the social media platform

Facebook faced criticism for its data handling practices, highlighting the need for brands to navigate this fine line between providing personalized experiences and safeguarding user privacy. This challenge emphasizes the importance of establishing clear boundaries and ethical guidelines to ensure that hyper-personalization respects consumer autonomy and maintains trust while harnessing the power of AI and neuromarketing insights for tailored brand experiences.

AUTHOR'S NOTE

The future of Brand Psychology is characterized by the integration of advanced technologies and psychological insights. This evolution involves leveraging artificial intelligence, advanced analytics, and neuroscience to gain a thorough understanding of consumer behaviour. Machine learning algorithms will analyse extensive data to predict trends, personalize experiences, and optimize branding strategies with high precision.

Ethical considerations will drive brand psychology practices, with transparent data collection and responsible use of persuasive techniques. Brands will need to focus on both consumer privacy and maintaining trust through ethical practices.

In the upcoming landscape, cultural sensitivity and inclusivity will be paramount. Brands will need to localize strategies to fit diverse cultural contexts and adopt inclusive practices that resonate with a broader audience.

Social responsibility will play a central role in brand strategies. Brands are expected not only to deliver quality products but also to address societal and environmental challenges. Ethical and sustainable practices will define successful brands.

Storytelling will remain pivotal, enhanced by technologies like virtual and augmented reality. These tools will enable brands to create immersive narratives that engage consumers on a deeper level.

The human connection will gain significance amidst the digital realm. Brands will focus on authenticity, fostering genuine relationships with consumers and using emotional branding to create lasting loyalty.

Consumer co-creation will be integral, as brands invite consumers to actively shape products and services. This collaborative approach will drive innovation and establish a sense of ownership among consumers.